The
Anatomy
of
Presence

I have had a lifelong pattern of running outside of myself for things like grounding, value, entertainment, and companionship. Now I have the choice at any given moment to live from my authentic inner location, and I no longer feel lonely and bored when I am by myself. As I stay in my core and radiate my presence outward, for the first time in my life I have effective boundaries with others that I can feel. In my professional work as a counselor, my presence with clients has become more immediate and effective.

Ildiko Overbay,
Licensed Professional Counselor, Oregon

Attention Strategies

The
Anatomy
of
Presence

Turn your inner authenticity
into outer impact and success

Glenn Hartelius, PhD
Michaela Aizer, CHT

The Anatomy of Presence
by
Glenn Hartelius and Michaela Aizer

Published by: Nicasio Press
                California, USA

ISBN: 979-8-9897756-4-4

CONTENTS

INTRODUCTION

Attention is the new currency of the twenty-first century. Everyone and everything wants a piece of your attention. In order to be effective, we have to stretch attention across work, family, social media, news, friends, and much more. When burn-out hits, we turn to exercise, music, yoga, positive thinking, or other practices, distractions, and entertainments that give the body and nervous system enough rest and renewal to re-engage with the demands. These are all useful tools, but they are only part of the answer—and restoration of energy is only part of the problem.

The daily struggle to manage many kinds of tasks, an endless stream of information, and ever-changing relationships can fill our inner space so much that we begin to lose the sense of ourselves. We can be so busy putting attention on this job and that conversation that we lose touch with why we are doing all of this and what it all means. Alongside the push to manage life is the desire to know ourselves more authentically, and to find more meaning in our relationships, careers, and lives.

Yet there is more to life and leadership than coping with demands and uncovering meaning. Mastery is not just about collecting information—it is also about finding and using states of mind that are attuned to our tasks. A state of quiet absorption may create flow for a project requiring sustained attention to detail but will not be optimal for interpersonal conversation or collaboration. Sustained high performance requires discerning which high-level inner states are suited for each area of work and life and then learning how to access them quickly.

Attention Strategies bring new ways to renew energy and attention, find sources of meaning, as well as find and access the high-level states that excellence requires. It is about how to become intimately acquainted with your attention—with the part of you that is looking for answers. We are so busy putting our attention on external things that it never occurs to us to notice where our attention is coming from. When we discover its source inside of us, how it shapes itself within body and mind, we can learn to cultivate it and have it in abundance.

Attention Strategies will not take you to some extraordinary place outside of yourself, or some exalted mystical state of consciousness. Attention Strategies are for finding your way back to your natural self—the parts of your mind that have always been yours but may have been misplaced and forgotten due to life's pressures and demands.

As children, we have the sense that we are growing and maturing. With the busy responsibilities of adult life, that satisfying feeling of developing as a person may be lost, and it may feel as if the mind is slowly filling with information and responsibilities, leaving less and less room for us to live and breathe. Distractions are attractive because they allow us to escape for a little while, but afterwards we find ourselves back in our cluttered, everyday minds.

Your everyday mind has lost touch with the rest of you, but by recovering whole of the natural mind, you can regain that sense of inner growth and renewal. Attention Strategies mentor you into reconnecting with all the parts of yourself —all of your capacities, resources, histories, challenges, and wisdom—so you can integrate them into an experience of self that is emotionally whole and focused.

How does this happen? Notice the attention you are using to read this sentence—the attention you gather behind your eyes, that you energize and direct outward so you can "focus" on the words. But where does your attention come from? Where is its point of origin? That point, where your attention comes from, is you.

That is the mystery. Finding that point, that source where your attention flows from, is the opening to a whole inner world—your world. This is where your skills and gifts are—the ones you know about, and the ones you have not yet discovered. Here is your intuition, your creativity, and your inspiration. As you map out this world and learn to navigate, you gain access to your inner strengths and the skills to express them more effectively through your work and your relationships.

The map that Attention Strategies will guide you to create is not some concept or metaphor. It is a new and different kind of map, a practical map you can use to directly access these powerful inner resources. This map is different because it is written in the language of the body, not the language of the everyday thinking mind.

The everyday mind is the one that you use to remember where your keys are and all the things you need to do today. It is the mind that your schoolwork and professional training have taught you to use. This mind is always busy and always talking to itself. Because your destination is not in the ordinary mind, teaching methods based in the ordinary mind cannot take you there. Only a different kind of map can bring you to the inner resources you are looking for.

Using your head—your everyday thinking mind—helps you get ahead, for a while. But at a certain point you begin to sense that you've left vital parts of yourself behind … and you won't be your best self until you get your whole self back.

Attention Strategies open the way to become more *you*, to move from your everyday mind to the core of your being so you can grow and unfold and develop yourself and your capacities in a way that feels natural. When you use Attention Strategies to connect quietly and deeply with your inner self, and live *as your inner self*, others will also feel the shift in your presence. Those around you will experience you differently, and you will have greater impact on them.

This book will show you how to experience:

- What it feels like to find your attention and inhabit your body
- How to cultivate your natural, quietly focused mind
- Where and how to find an authentic experience of gratitude
- The actual sensations of living from your deepest self
- What it is like to find quiet satisfaction with your life in this moment
- How to unleash the power and impact of your whole-person presence

Whether you want to enhance your ability to hold a room during meetings or presentations, build your leadership presence in daily interactions, become a more effective listener who is able to create a safe space, improve your ability to find and sustain mental focus, access your intuitive and creative capacities, learn to inspire yourself and others, or just access a quieter and more peaceful state of mind within yourself, these Attention Strategies will show you how, with simple language and easy step-by-step instructions—and using the part of you that is reading this sentence right now: your attention.

How do we know this? These attentional strategies are based on work with thousands of clients and on groundbreaking research by our team of renowned scientists. There are many claims that some new work is "revolutionary," but we have achieved something genuinely new. For more than a hundred years, psychologists have tried to measure consciousness—and our team has finally succeeded: we have demonstrated the ability to measure specific states of consciousness.

These studies demonstrate scientifically that with precise descriptions, we are able to teach high-performance states rapidly and effectively. For example, in one of our studies we were able to teach beginners a state that was highly effective in reducing stress and increasing mindfulness in just thirty minutes. These are skills that usually take weeks or months to learn.

This is not just one new finding among the hundreds that are made every year—this is a game-changing achievement that opens the way for an entirely new area of psychology, with powerful skills for daily life. This is not just a new discovery, but a new type of discovery Because these findings are based directly on measurements of brain activity and precisely described experiences, we have been able to create tools that make direct, powerful changes in your wellbeing, in your skills, and in your happiness.

With this new integral approach to psychology, we are able to use objective scientific measurement to discover states of consciousness very much like those used by great traditions such as Buddhism, and describe them in ways that make them easy to learn.

This is not another way to share ancient teachings— though our findings appear to overlap with some traditional wisdom. It is the creation of entirely new ways to regulate consciousness. Here we use inner states not just for meditation but to develop excellence in our personal and professional lives with skills that go far beyond meditation.

These tools do not require giving up one's life and immersing in years of practice, as traditional approaches once did. This work is suited to our way of life in industrialized cultures, so we can gain the benefits of traditional practices in ways that are compatible with contemporary life. New descriptions of attention and presence that are both easy to access and scientifically tested open that door.

1.

A Silent Language of Impact

I was eighteen, shy, a socially awkward outsider who was curious about people who seemed to be endlessly attractive, in the center of attention, popular, noticed, and liked. They were a bit like famous film actors, whose star-power was worldwide. What did these people have? What gave them that sparkle that attracted those around them?

When I discovered that a celebrated actor would be appearing in a local theater production, I decided to attend and see what I could learn. With the cheapest ticket in hand for a matinee performance, I entered the grand theater, walked up the endless staircases to the highest balcony, and took my seat. I noticed at once that I was absolutely alone up there. The balcony was so high above the stage that the performers seemed tiny—I could barely discern their expressions, and their words were faint and muffled. "Well, that was a waste," I thought, as I resigned myself to watching little figures scurrying around on the stage for the rest of the play.

Then the curtains parted once more as a man entered the narrow stage, lifted his arm, and said something I couldn't make out. Though I had no idea what he said, it was as if a great wave swept up through the air, up the balconies, through me and past me—a wave that touched me, moved me, and lifted the hair on my neck and the back of my arms.

I said to myself, "That is Richard Burton, and that is why he is famous."

This was my first clear evidence that there is a silent language all of us use to affect each other without words. Consciously or not we sense each other's presence, our inner states of being communing wordlessly across the space between physical forms, powerfully shaping the nuances of personal and social relationships. Because of my shy, inward nature, I had not picked up these skills intuitively as a child, so I was driven to consciously seek out answers that others took for granted.

As experience and maturity brought me into the adult world with its social demands and responsibilities, this quest gained urgency. Gradually I built a capacity to perceive, track, and identify the process of how presence works, of how we communicate with each other through unspoken feeling qualities—messages that go well beyond conversation and ordinary social cues. I observed how the quality of one's presence predicts the response of those around them, and how those qualities can create rapport that connects, and that opens up creative and expansive conversation.

With time, through honing my ability to perceive the smallest details of the dynamics of human interaction and relationship, I was able to assess the qualities of presence of those around me. By presence I don't mean physical posture, body language, or the way words or voice is used. Presence is something that is felt but not seen—it is what you feel when someone who has it enters the room. It is an invisible language that is part of every conversation, every meeting, and every interaction—even when it is not noticed. Presence is what enables you to connect warmly with others, whether in a personal conversation over coffee, or in a presentation to a thousand people. Learning how to assess presence, and with time, how to cultivate presence, enabled me to be more at home, to own more of my personal location and power in the social and professional world.

Along the way I attended a conference presentation by a celebrated intuitive healer—a woman I admired as a serious communicator on the subject of inner healing, and whose presence would be informative to experience. The venue was a large conference room. I sat in row 33, near the back of the well-attended audience. The speaker was interesting and articulate, the sound system projected her voice well, and *I could not feel her at all*. I was surprised and disappointed—almost disoriented. Then I recalled that she was relatively new to public speaking. Perhaps the size of this venue was unfamiliar to her—perhaps she had not developed the skill to fill such a large physical space. It was new to think of presence as something that could have a physical size, but there was a way to find out! I left my seat in row 33 and slowly walked down the aisle toward the stage. At row 16 I felt her—a radiant, inspiring presence that was everything I had expected. I was grateful to her for teaching me this:

The invisible dynamics of presence seem to have physical size and shape.

This discovery was to become central: that unseen dynamics of presence that shape relationship are *located*, and can be experienced and described much the same way as a flower or a dress or a piece of furniture.

But this insight came much later in my journey. At the time of my encounter with Richard Burton, I was apprenticing in archeology as a volunteer. Uncovering the ancient past attracted me because it represented uncovering hidden knowledge and getting to the bottom of things—in quite a literal way. After years of excavating in the ruins of an ancient city in the Middle East and completing my coursework, I received a master's degree in religious studies. But by then I suspected that sorting ancient pottery was not going to bring me to the deep understandings I wanted.

I headed in a new direction, and chose to explore the human story along a completely different pathway— therapeutic massage and hands-on healing work. My academic community was stunned that I would turn away from my successes; my parents were aghast. I assured them that this was just an interim, a stop along the way. In fact, it was the very education I needed to guide me into a deeper understanding of fine distinctions in presence. It was through this work that I came to understand that

The mind is in the whole body.

Yet this "body" that the mind inhabits is not some second-class citizen, not the dutiful downstairs servants' quarters of a mind-body connection, but the aspect of mind that opens new creative leaps of mastery after the intellect has topped out at the summit of its knowledge. That insight was still far in the future.

About five years into my professional work with the body, I had several experiences that initiated a profound shift my views about mind, body, and spirit.

Working as a body therapist, I began to pay attention to sensations that arose in my body as I first met clients and found that I could often feel where their injuries were by noticing reflected sensations in my body: *these sensations in my body led me to where I would find injuries in their body.* How was this possible, I wondered. No book I had read or subject I had studied—including psychology—had ever described ways that information could be transmitted from one person to another without words or cues that one could see. The skeptical part of my mind wondered how this could be real. The intuitive side was intrigued.

An insight came some months later. I noticed that as I worked with clients, something changed: their breathing movements shifted from the chest down to the belly. They relaxed deeply, and the felt quality in the room shifted. It was as if *some thing* moved downward in their bodies. I decided to see whether I could consciously encourage this shift—feeling that if I could get this *something* to move in my client, using only my intention and without touching the client, then perhaps this notion was more than just my imagination. When I tried it, my client, who was face-down on the table, relaxed immediately. His breathing shifted from his chest to his belly—*and I had not even touched him.* I drew back, astounded that the exercise had worked. It showed me that

Bodies communicate with each other using the invisible language of relationship.

These experiences were my first glimpses of natural abilities that each person has, once the intelligence and intuitions of their whole body are awakened. In this natural state, it is possible to *feel* information that is arriving, wordlessly and invisibly, from others through qualities of presence. Through experimentation and study of my experiences as well as poring through a library of books and articles about this frontier, this became clear: I had encountered:

An embodied state of consciousness.

"Embodied" refers to the fact that in some states, there is more awareness of the whole body, and *in* the whole body.

Even though I had developed a reliable way to bring my clients into this embodied state of being, and of entering into this state with them, I still did not know how to consciously access it for myself. One day, as I passed a mirror in the hallway of our home, something caught my eye—and I stopped. In a flash, it was as if I "saw" in the mirror, and in the same moment, felt, a point in the middle of my head—a point where "I" was located. I thought, "Oh, this is interesting—it's as if the 'I' that is me has an actual *location* in my head." I wondered whether it might be possible to move this "I" location down into my body.

Perhaps I could move this down in the same way I had moved the "something" down in my client's body. This was a fascinating possibility!

I stood in front of the mirror and concentrated my gaze on the reflection of this imagined point, while also feeling the point in the middle of my head. Then I imagined I could move it slowly downward.

To my utter amazement, *something moved.* Or, more precisely, *I moved.*

The stable sense of self that was located in my head shifted downward with this imagined point. The "I" that looked out of my eyes and listened through my ears was now located an inch lower than it had been a moment before. Thrilled but wary, I continued moving myself down through the head, through the neck, and several inches down into my chest. Then I stopped, daring to go no farther.

As I moved down into the body,
my sense of self changed radically.

Everything went quiet. My thoughts stopped, yet I was no less aware of what was happening. This fact alone surprised me—for I had no idea it was possible to be conscious without thinking; I thought thinking *was* consciousness. Yet here I was, completely silent inside, and still fully aware of what was happening. If anything, my senses were sharpened because they were free from the constant conversation in my head.

"Is this what happens in meditation?" I asked myself.

I had tried to learn meditation a few times, but found the instructions confusing. To be honest, I had no patience to spend months practicing something I could not feel, in the hope that one day I would get there. Yet here I was presented with a different scenario. If shifting to a quiet state of mind was as simple as finding the "I" located in my head and moving it down into the body, I realized that I could accomplish this shift into an embodied state in a much more direct way—without having to practice for weeks or months.

And I could use this state in my everyday life.

But characterizing these skills as "meditation" is wholly inadequate. It would be akin to characterizing gold as "just that tooth-repair metal." While certain kinds of meditation have been shown to increase wellbeing, reduce stress, improve attention, and enhance mood, meditation is generally thought of as something that creates benefit by *turning off the mind.* Silencing the mind is often understood as some kind of limbo that allows the brain to rest so it can function better when you turn it back on. This is far from the reality.

When you use these states, they quiet one part of the mind, while energizing other parts of your intelligence.

There are stacks of books that describe the "something more" that comes with mastery, with genius, with intuition. These states don't just create peace by turning off the endless yak-yak of the thinking mind, *they turn on the creative magic of "Aha!"*

If you feel you've hit a ceiling after mastering the language and the skills of your profession, your sport, your art, or your business, that next level will not come by filling your head with more facts and information. *It will come as you enliven the inner resources that inhabit this quiet, unassuming sphere of your intelligence.* This enlivening comes from using the high-level states that Attention Strategies introduce.

What I happened onto that day in front of the mirror was not something mysterious or esoteric. It was so obvious, so "right here" in my experience, that I had never noticed it. In that same way, these resources are *right here* in your experience, waiting to be noticed and awakened. The key that unlocks this inner door is:

Attention.

Not just attention in the sense of what you *focus on* in the outside world, but also in terms of *where your attention comes from*, inside your experience.

Change where your attention comes from, and you change your state of mind.

To change where your attention comes from, you don't need to sit quietly; you don't need to believe in something or someone; you don't need to wear special clothes, practice postures, or repeat words from an ancient language. Any of these practices can be beneficial, but *you don't need them in order to gain mastery of your inner states and access to game-changing personal resources.*

Attention Strategies are simple processes that empower you to change your state of mind whenever you want, to access the resources you need.

A good example is *presence*, which is having a bit of a moment. Think of presence as a quality that radiates out from a person, a human version of light shining from a bulb —a quality that communicates something about who they are. Presence can increase your ability to connect, impact, guide, and lead. It is easy to understand the value of presence but harder to generate, or even say what it actually is. If "presence" means that something is here, what is it that is present?

The answer is simple:

Attention is the source of presence—
so attention is what is "present."

Attention creates presence, perceives presence, regulates presence, and navigates presence.

Manage your attention, and you have control of
your presence.

Unlike light from a lightbulb, human presence has texture. It holds feelings you are feeling right now, feelings from the past, information about your state of being, and patterns from old ways of being. Attention not only powers presence, it opens the way for using presence to heal inner wounds and change hardened ways of being.

It begins with the experience of finding your own attention, then learning how to move it. You will know when attention lands in your body and you connect with the sensation of being "in." When it happens, it is as clear as a blue sky. You will know because the mind quiets to less than a whisper, awareness expands into that quiet, and the world feels different.

Those who use Attention Strategies around the world, from students to yoga teachers to business leaders, have had that moment—that surprise of shifted awareness, almost like the clink of a mechanism locking in place, and the pleasurable sensation of landing more deeply in the body.

Come along and find out for yourself.

2.

FIND YOUR ATTENTION

You may have heard of mind maps, but Attention Strategies offer you a new and different way to map the mind. Years ago, I bought a book about mind maps, one that offered a wonderful compilation of scores of ideas about the structure of mind. I bought it because I had not yet created my own maps, and given my struggles finding my way to social fluency, I thought that having an actual *map* of the mind might be of some help.

To me, a map is something that offers easy-to-read patterns of how the important parts of something are arranged. A map of a microprocessor shows patterns of circuit pathways as I might see them through a powerful microscope, and a street map of San Francisco depicts the patterns of roadways as they might look from the air. Maps of brain function show which parts of the brain are active with various kinds of stimulation and activity. Here was a book that claimed to map not just the brain, but the *mind*. I was fascinated to see what such a map might look like.

As I studied the book, I was disappointed to find no maps of the mind at all. There were maps of the *brain* and drawings that illustrated *ideas* about the mind. There were no mind-maps of the sort I had wished for—no diagrams of mental structure that might help me with *the mind that I experience.*

The maps in this book are practical maps, maps of the mind as you find it *in here*, inside your own experience. It is an anatomy of the mind that shows you, not how the brain is organized, not how ideas of the mind are organized, but how *your experience* of the mind is organized *in the space of your body*. In other words, *it is a map you can use to find your way around your own mind*.

Who is the "you" that finds its way around your mind? *It's your attention*. Attention is the you that is reading this sentence, right now. This attention has a location in your body—likely in your head. When you learn how to shift your attention down into your body, a new world opens. In this new location, there is more room to be present with yourself and with the contents of your mind. Here there is more information than you might imagine about you, about the people you engage with, and about the world around you. In this quieter, more spacious place, you will find the controls for effectively regulating your mind, your focus, your resilience, your connections with others, and your presence. This location is an entirely different way of being *you*.

Tom, the CEO of a small company, had just come off of a very important call with every employee in the firm, sharing a positive milestone. The call went well, but in his body he still felt the weight of the responsibility he held while making that announcement to the whole company. He felt drained and had considered taking the rest of the day off to recover. Instead, by moving his attention into the core of his body and adopting the inner stance of leadership, he was able to feel the weight releasing and his natural energy returning. By changing his inner stance, he rapidly felt restored, ready to continue work as usual.

Helen, an executive coach who trusted her own expertise in her subject matter, knew there was something missing in her practice: she was not connecting with her clients the way she wanted to. By learning and using the attentional stance for creating presence, safe space, and cultivating rapport, she began to experience a new level of satisfaction in her work.

Andile, the CEO of a small consulting firm, was about to give his first keynote presentation to a large audience. He knew his content was good, but he was nervous about having impact. He wanted to be taken seriously. By practicing and using the attentional stance for leadership presence, he was able to connect powerfully with the audience so they not only heard him, they *felt* him. He hit it out of the park.

In this chapter you will discover how to find your attention. In a later chapter, you will learn how to move it down into the space of your body. Entering this new world is just the beginning. As we explore this territory together, you may find your way to skills and abilities that may have seemed out of reach, or discover tools to enhance the gifts you have and feel more confident in your ability to develop and use them consistently.

It all begins with noticing what it is like to be yourself in an ordinary way. For many of us, this means being in the head much of the time. Being in your head can be like standing in a crowded elevator where everyone is talking at once, with a dozen conversations competing for your attention.

This does not have to be the normal *you*. You can learn to be in your body. The head is part of the body too, but here I will use *body* to refer to the trunk of the body—chest, back, belly, and pelvis—where emotions and feelings are actually felt. Being in your body is like sitting quietly at a poolside table, reading a book, or having a conversation: there is room to hold a comfortable overview while focusing on the particular task at hand.

Notice Where Your Attention Comes From

How you get from the head down into the body is simple: find your attention and move it into the space of your body. Finding your attention includes coming to understand the experience of attention in a different way— as something that is located at a specific place in the human body. In psychology, attention is a cognitive process where you focus on one part of what is around you and ignore everything else. If someone asks you, "Where is your attention?" you might say, "My attention is on the cat." You have selectively concentrated your attention on some part of your experience.

Yet notice that attention has two poles. On one end is what your attention is *pointed at.* You might shift your attention from texts on your phone to the face of a person sitting in front of you, then to the color of their jacket. On the other end is the place your attention *comes from,* in your body. This is the part of attention that is rarely noticed—the part inside the body where the noticing is coming from. Despite being overlooked, this source or seat of your attention is central to your ability to access all of your inner resources. Especially important is *where* the seat of your attention is located.

It is commonly believed that attention comes from the head, since that is where the brain is, and where most sense organs are located—eyes, ears, mouth, and nose. In cartoons, thought bubbles come from the head because that is where the "I" who is thinking seems to be located. Some people even have the experience of being a little person inside their own head, a little person who looks out through their eyes and listens through their ears. It is as if this little person runs the control room inside their head.

Imagine you are hiking in a wilderness area, and you come to a big sign with a trail map. It might strike you as impressive that a team of people hauled in sign-building materials to a spot that is hours from the nearest road. As you scan the map, one of the first things you'll need to look for is the place that says, "You are here." Without this information, the map is pretty much useless—you can't use the map to get where you want to go unless you know where you are.

In the case of Attention Strategies, *your body is the map you will use* to find different kinds of internal resources. Finding your attention is how you discover where you are on your body map.

The way you find the "I am here" location on your body map is by noticing *where you are noticing from.* Where does the information go after it arrives through your eyes or your ears? When you ask yourself a question, where is the part of you that is listening to the question? Many readers will feel the information arriving to an "I" that seems to be located in the head. Others may feel they are receiving the words somewhere in the chest, in the general region of the heart. There is no right or wrong location, just the experience of noticing that "I" is located here, at a particular place in the body.

FIND YOUR ATTENTION

As you read this sentence, say to yourself, "I am reading this sentence," and notice that you are, indeed, reading it. You will be using your eyes to read, but notice where the "I" is who gets the information from your vision. Where do the words from the page arrive? At your knees? Your elbows? Your low back? Your chest? Your head? Where is the part of you that is wondering whether you are doing the exercise correctly? Where the "I" receives the words, or asks yourself a question, is where your attention is located.

Where your attention sits at a particular time is your *attentional stance.* Just as you can stand up straight, sit back in a chair, kneel on a bench, or lie on the floor, you can hold your attention in different stances. *Noticing where your noticing happens* is how you find your attention—it is the felt experience of the "I" who receives your sensations and manages your experience.

Here is another exercise:

LOCATE YOUR LISTENER

Stop reading for a moment and listen to the sounds around you. Do you hear someone speaking? the noise of cars? the sound of a heater, a fan, or the wind? Notice where you feel the sounds arriving to your body. Do they seem to land in your head through the ears? your chest? somewhere else in your body? Where you sense the sounds landing is where your attention is located.

In the next chapter you will be able to take a simple test that will help you determine whether you tend to sit in your head or in your heart, and discover how each of these attentional stances shapes your personality.

3.

Use Your Head, Follow Your Heart

"Head" and "heart" are often used to describe the emotional quality of a person or an action, with "head" representing thought, the intellect, and reason, and "heart" reflecting emotion, feeling, and passion. For example, someone who is "in their head a lot" is considered intellectually bright but perhaps disconnected from their emotions. On the other hand, a "gift from the heart" is one offered with strong emotional feelings.

These are not just metaphors. There is good evidence that where one's self is located has an impact on personality and decision-making. But before sharing this information with you, I invite you to take a short assessment that will help you decide whether your usual location is in your head or in your heart.

This little quiz was one I created together with one of my doctoral students—she is now Dr. Marie Sester—to help determine whether someone tends to "use their head" or "follow their heart." In the language of Attention Strategies, this is the difference between an attentional stance in the head or in the heart area of the chest.

IS YOUR ATTENTIONAL STANCE IN THE HEAD OR THE HEART?

Please set aside your knowledge of biological facts, and choose one answer to each question that feels right.

1. Which of the following maxims do you consider to carry more importance in life:
    a. Follow your heart
    b. Only cheaters prosper
    c. Only the good die young
    d. Use your head

2. Which of the following do you consider a better characterization of how you function in the world:
    a. Indecisive and frozen
    b. Rational and logical
    c. Intuitive and feeling
    d. Impulsive and reactive

3. Which factors are more important in moral decision-making processes:
    a. Intuitive and feeling factors
    b. Financial gains
    c. Selfish considerations
    d. Rational considerations

4. Which of the following do you think would be a more accurate reflection of how others might characterize your interpersonal style:
    a. Interpersonally combative
    b. Interpersonally reserved
    c. Interpersonally warm
    d. Interpersonally indifferent

5. When you care about someone, where in your body do you think the caring comes from:
   a. Heart
   b. Gut
   c. Somewhere else or don't know
   d. Brain

6. Which of the following locations do you think of as the location of your "self"?
   a. Gut
   b. Brain
   c. Heart
   d. Somewhere else or don't know

7. When you feel close to someone, where in your body do you feel the closeness?
   a. Heart
   b. Somewhere else or don't know
   c. Gut
   d. Brain

8. When you feel authentic, or true to yourself, where in your body do you feel the authenticity?
   a. Gut
   b. Brain
   c. Heart
   d. Somewhere else or don't know

9. When you feel empathy for someone, where in your body do you feel the empathy?
   a. Heart
   b. Gut
   c. Somewhere else or don't know
   d. Brain

10. Which aspect of you carries the strongest influence in making important decisions?
    a. Gut
    b. Brain
    c. Heart
    d. Somewhere else or don't know

11. Which aspect of you carries the strongest influence in experiencing beauty?
    a. Heart
    b. Somewhere else or don't know
    c. Gut
    d. Brain

12. When you feel a strong conviction about something, where in your body is the conviction coming from?
    a. Gut
    b. Brain
    c. Heart
    d. Somewhere else or don't know

13. When you feel a strong connection with someone, where in your body do you sense the connection?
    a. Heart
    b. Gut
    c. Somewhere else or don't know
    d. Brain

14. When it comes to knowing, which part of the body do you trust the most?
    a. Somewhere else or don't know
    b. Brain
    c. Heart
    d. Gut

Scoring:

1. Count up the number of times you selected "a" as the answer on odd-numbered questions (1, 3, 5, 7, …).
2. Count up the number of times you selected "c" as the answer on even-numbered questions (2, 4, 6, 8, …).
3. Add together the results from step 1 and step 2. This is your "A" number.
4. Count up the number of times you selected "b" as the answer on even-numbered questions (2, 4, 6, 8, …).
5. Count up the number of times you selected "d" as the answer on odd-numbered questions (1, 3, 5, 7, …).
6. Add together the results from step 4 and step 5. This is your "B" number.
7. Subtract your "B" number from your "A" number—the answer can be a negative number. This is your final score.

If your score is between 4 and 14, your attentional stance is probably in the heart. If your score is between -4 and -14, your attentional stance is likely to be in the head. If your score is between 3 and -3, you may use both attentional stances.

For example, if you selected "a" as the answer to 4 odd-numbered questions and "c" as the answer to 6 even-numbered questions, then you would add these scores together: (4 + 6 = 10)—this is your "A" number. Then if you selected "b" as the answer on 1 even-numbered question and "d" as an answer on 3 odd-numbered questions, you would add these together for your "B" number: (1 + 3 = 4). Subtract your "B" number from your "A" number to get your final score (10 − 4 = 6). Since this score is between 4 and 14, your usual attentional stance is likely to be in the heart area of the chest.

As you read through the differences that have been found between people who self-locate in the head and those who self-locate in the heart, remember that here is no right or wrong way to be. Also keep in mind that not every person who locates themselves in a particular way will have all the characteristics associated with the groups that were measured.

It turns out that people who think of themselves as located in the head are more rational and logical and more likely to be emotionally reserved. They are also likely to think of the brain as the organ associated with caring, closeness, empathy, and the perception of beauty. Head-located individuals are less likely to try to be agreeable with others and less likely to have spiritual interests.

People who feel that they are located in the heart tend to be more warm, more emotional, and more likely to value feelings. They are likely to think of the heart as the organ of caring, closeness, empathy, and the experience of beauty. They are more likely to try to create harmony with others and more likely to be interested in spirituality.

One might explain this by saying that people who are more logical and rational naturally pick "head" as their metaphor, and people who are more emotional relate to "heart," because those are the usual associations. For example, one study found that the people who identified the head as their location had higher grade point averages in school and better general knowledge than those who identified with being in the heart. Also, heart-located individuals solved difficult moral problems based on emotional rather than logical considerations. Both of these facts could be explained by suggesting that people identify with the metaphor that best represented their preferences and strengths.

But another study with a different set of participants found that people who merely pointed to their heads while answering general knowledge questions scored higher than those who pointed to their hearts while answering the same questions. Similarly, heart-pointers solved moral dilemmas in a more emotional manner than head-pointers. It seemed as though just pointing to head or heart could make a person either smarter or more emotional.

None of this makes sense in ordinary terms. How could people get smarter by pointing to their heads and more emotional by pointing to their hearts? The researchers who conducted these studies proposed that being "in the head" or "in the heart" was just metaphorical. But it is hard to imagine that just changing metaphors or pointing to some body part could improve knowledge or increase dependence on emotion.

A better explanation is that a person's choice of metaphor represented their actual attentional stance, and that pointing to the head or the heart caused them to temporarily shift their attentional stance. Our research team has found that each attentional stance creates a distinct pattern of brain activity, so:

> *You can use your attentional stance*
> *to control your brain states.*

If this is true, then what if you could learn to change your attentional stance so your knowledge skills could be better when you need them, and then when you need stronger emotional intelligence, you could move to the attentional stance associated with emotional strengths? Each attentional stance would optimize your brain function for a particular type of task.

Finding out whether you are located in the head or in the heart is like a fun personality test, but what makes it better than a way to find out what "type" you are is realizing that *you can adjust your access to various aspects of yourself to fit your needs.* You can bring forward the inner resources to support different skillsets, *just by changing your attentional stance.*

Attention Strategies bring a detailed body map, along with clear and direct instructions that show you exactly how to shift your inner attentional stance. The key is precision. When you need to use a map to get somewhere, a watercolor map that offers soft-hued impressions of the journey may be beautiful but hard to use for navigation. A map with precise features and easy-to-understand directions works much better.

As an example of how precision instructions make all the difference, a friend of mine shared with me the story of a basketball coach who accomplished incredible things with a junior basketball team. The coach—we will call him Ralph—used to play for a major professional sports franchise, and word had it that if he coached one of the teams in the league, you might as well hand them the championship trophy at the beginning of the season—he was that good.

Ralph took on the job of coaching a team in a California resort area where my friend lived. The first day he lined the kids up and said, "Let's see you do lay-ups." One by one the kids dribbled the ball down the court and leaped up to lay the ball into the basket. Some of them had been playing basketball for years and were able to do a fair-to-middling lay-up.

Then there was Larry. Larry was the fat kid who had never been good at any sport. He was the kind of kid who got to be the butt of every joke and who spent most of the season on the bench. When Larry dribbled the ball down the court and tried to do a lay-up, his arms, legs, and the ball flew in five different directions.

When Ralph saw Larry's performance, he instructed the rest of the team to keep on practicing lay-ups. Then he took Larry to the next court to show him a few things. "This is how you flex your fingers," Ralph said, as he moved Larry's chubby digits in just the right way, "and this is how you pivot your wrist." In a few minutes of precise, joint-by-joint instruction, Larry learned how to move his hand without the basketball, then with the basketball. Then Ralph showed him how to move his arm, first without the ball, then with the ball. Finally Ralph showed him how to jump up on one foot, then how to jump up on one foot while moving his hand and arm.

"Okay," Ralph told him, "now I want you to run down to that line just below the basket and stop." Larry ran and stopped. "Now come back here and run down again, and when you get to the line, I want you to jump up and move your arm the way I showed you." Larry ran and jumped. "Alright, now I want you to run down while you dribble the ball, jump up and push the ball toward the basket." Larry ran, dribbled, jumped, and laid the ball neatly into the basket.

Because of Ralph's precise, practical, step-by-step instructions on *exactly* how to use his body, Larry was able to shoot baskets as well as anyone on the team, and play in the championship game—which they won.

Okay, so it is probably clear that where your attention comes from—the *seat* of your attention—has a location in your body, and from the test in this chapter, you likely have a sense of where in your body you tend to sit most often. What may be less clear is *what an attentional stance feels like.*

In the next chapter, you will learn your first attentional stance—how to bring your mind to a state of quiet mental focus.

4.

QUIET MENTAL FOCUS

Now that you have a sense of where your attention sits in your body, you will be able to *move to a new attentional stance*. The first of these will likely be familiar: the stance of focused mind. As you move out of your familiar inner stance to a new one, your sense of what an attentional stance is will become more clear.

Focusing the mind offers a perfect example of how the inner structure of attention is usually overlooked: people who already know how to focus their attention do it without thinking. Those who do not know struggle to figure out how to focus with little guidance from others, usually in the form of vague instructions that are only helpful if you already know how. People who have not learned the internal steps to create mental focus are not likely to learn them by being told to, "pay attention!" As a result, even quite intelligent individuals who struggle to focus may feel that they are "just not smart enough."

A step-by-step attention strategy for precisely how to focus attention is in itself something that has the potential for powerful impact in education as well as on productivity. For example, for a couple of years at the start of my work teaching in psychology, I taught general psych courses at a community college in an economically depressed neighborhood close to San Francisco. At the end of the first lecture, I assigned some pages of reading and told students to be ready for a quiz at the start of the next class. Malcolm was slumped so far down in his seat that his legs extended well beyond the desk. In response to the assignment he called out, "How are we supposed to do that?" I realized that he was not expressing an attitude or trying to disrupt the class; he was telling me that he did not know how to read a textbook in a way that would prepare him for testing on the contents.

I asked him to stay for a few minutes after class, and he walked with me to a quiet office. He had been using a very different attentional stance—one that would relay information about safety in his environment but would make it difficult to take in and retain knowledge about a school subject. I showed him a simple, step-by-step strategy for moving from his scanning-for-safety stance to a focused-mind stance—one that would allow him to learn from his textbook. Then I asked him to read a paragraph from the textbook. All he said was, "Oh."

I came to the next class hoping he would return. He was there. He passed the quiz, passed the quizzes and tests that followed, and earned a B+ in the course—at least in part because *he grasped the attention strategy for mental focus.* Teaching him this strategy only took a few minutes, and once he had it, he was able to put it to use on his own without further instruction. He had the ability, he just needed the right tool.

If focusing comes easily for you, the following exercise will be a different way to arrive at a familiar location. If you are one of those who struggles with focus, even this preliminary step may be helpful in strengthening a necessary skill.

The tool you will use to focus your mind is an *internal sensation*. A simple exercise will show you how to create this kind of sensation, that we will then use for mental focus.

CREATE AN INTERNAL SENSATION

With one finger, lightly touch the back of your other hand, then lift your finger away. See if you can feel where the touch was. If the sensation goes away quickly, try touching again, more lightly.

I find that many people are able to feel where the touch was, even after lifting their finger away. If you don't feel the sensation, imagine that your finger has created a bright point of light where it touched your skin.

Now, imagine that the sensation on the back of your hand is a little point of light. Imagine that the point of light moves about half an inch on the surface of your hand. As you see the point of light moving in your imagination, what happens to the sensation? Pause for a moment, and notice what you feel.

For some people, the sensation moves with the point of light. For others, the sensation gets wider, so it is in both places.

This exercise shows that touch may be a two-way process. Instead of the usual notion that touch is just information going from the skin to the brain, the fact that the sensation on the back of the hand moves and changes suggests that there is also a way that the mind can create an experience of touch on the skin. This ability to create a sensation is what will be used in the next exercise, which enables you to focus your attention.

Have you ever found yourself avoiding what you really need to do, getting lost in a social media app, snacking, or doing one household chore after another so you can distract yourself from the task you know you want to finish? Creating mental focus can help you cut through the avoidance and quiet the distractions so you can concentrate on what you need to do.

FOCUS YOUR ATTENTION (FIG. 4.1)

Use one finger to lightly touch the top of your head right at the crown or center, then lift the finger away. Feel for the sensation that stays after your finger has lifted. Imagine you can still feel this sensation. If it is helpful, imagine it as a small point of light on top of your head.

Now imagine that this point slowly sinks down into your head. Watch the image in your imagination, or feel the sensation as it moves. Allow the point to sink down several inches (4–6 cm), so it ends up in the middle of your head behind your eyes.

Imagine that you are this point in the center of your head. Rather than being the head that notices the point at its center, become the point that notices the head.

Notice each of the sounds around you, and imagine these sounds are arriving at your ears, then coming in to where you are in the center of your head. As you inhale, feel yourself as the point that draws the breath to itself, and releases it back out. If your eyes are closed, allow them to open with soft focus, and pretend the images come through your eyes and back to where you are in the center of your head.

Notice how the inside of your head feels. Notice how much conversation is happening in your mind. Notice whether or not you feel clear and focused.

As variations, you can try touching a point on the center of the forehead or on the center of the back of your head, then guiding the sensation into the center of your head from either of those locations. These approaches work well for some individuals. There is also another alternate exercise near the end of this chapter.

Figure 4.1

Mental focus is not just about what happens at the other end of attention—the end that is pointed at something—it is about what happens at the place the attention comes from. When attention sits in the whole head, there is a constant inner conversation. "Where did I put my keys. Oh, here they are. Why did I put them here? Oh well. What was I doing? Right, the letter to Johnson. I was supposed to do this yesterday. OK, what was this about?..." and on and on it goes, often all day long. This inner chatter can be exhausting, distracting, and an obstacle to quiet, consistent productivity.

For many people, attention sits like a cloud in the whole head, which makes mental focus feel like an effort. If you imagine lightning going off every few seconds in that cloud as one thought after another lights up inside the mind, you get a good picture of a pretty typical everyday mind. What is remarkable is that people are able to function as well as they do with a noisy, cluttered mind.

The process of bringing a loose cloud of attention into an imagined point of light in the middle of the head *is the act of focusing the mind*. When attention is focused in the center of the head, the mind becomes quiet and attentive, ready to concentrate and take in information. Note that this is not attention focused *on* the middle of the head, it is attention focused *from* the middle of the head.

The Feeling of Location

A white-knuckle ride on a corkscrew roller coaster can be exhilarating when you can "hold onto yourself" internally. When I was a teenager living wholly in my head, any intense ride left me feeling ill for hours—because I did not know how to manage my attention.

When I was in my early 30s and just beginning to have a sense of how to regulate my attention, a visiting relative from Europe wanted to visit a theme park that had dozens of stomach-churning rides. I found that by keeping my attention sharply focused in the center of my body, I could hold myself together through even the wildest swings and twists. This skill served me well as life became more complex, and it was events that twisted and turned.

Focused presence, whether in the head or heart, creates a felt sense of *"Ah, here I am."* The sensate experience of one's own location helps in navigating the daily maze of texts, posts, emails, calls, advertisements, news, computers, phones, tablets, smart televisions, and voice assistants. These "conveniences" have an unquenchable thirst for human attention, and their nonstop stimulation draws the mind away from this simple, grounding experience of, *"Oh yes, this is me."*

Even when the body-felt sense of self is at the edges of experience, it serves as an orienting reference point—a clear but subtle sense of *"this is me right here."* If this direct sense of self is lost—for example, if external stimulation is used to distract from uncomfortable feelings or avoid unpleasant tasks—inner location can be replaced by a sense of emptiness. More and stronger stimulation is then needed to avoid the lack of feeling. This cycle of avoidance or dependence on distraction can be interrupted quickly and effectively by displacing it with a direct experience of focused attention.

Here is an alternate way to create the experience of focused attention in your head:

ANOTHER WAY TO FOCUS YOUR ATTENTION (FIG. 4.2)

Rub the palms of your hands together for 10–20 seconds, then close your eyes and bring your hands slowly toward your face. Gently contact your whole face with your open palms and fingers, then repeat the same gentle contact on the sides of your face, the sides of your head, the back of your head, and the top of your head—each time imagining that you can still feel where your hands touched you after you lift them away.

Once you have touched your face and the sides and top of your head, imagine that you can feel the outline of your whole head. Now imagine that you can shrink this head-shaped sensation just a little, so that it fits inside of your actual head. This might make it about the size of a large grapefruit.

Now imagine that the sensation shrinks a little more, down to the size of an orange. Take a slow, comfortable breath, and imagine that it shrinks again, down to the size of a lime in the center of your head. After another easy, relaxed breath, imagine the sensation shrinks down to the size of a cherry. Imagine that there is a tiny, intensely bright light in the very center of the cherry, and imagine you can become that bright light.

As before, notice each of the sounds around you, and imagine these sounds are coming right through your ears, all the way to where you are in the center of your head. With each inhale, feel that you draw the breath in to where you are at the center of the head, then release it back out. Imagine that your eyes are windows that you can look through from where you sit in the center of your head.

Figure 4.2

This attentional stance focuses your mind in a way that makes sustained concentration much easier. If your work requires intellectual skills, this stance may make you better at your job or profession. It also gives you access to a felt sense of yourself, so necessary in the busy, overstimulated lives many of us manage on a daily basis.

5.

ATTENTIONAL CHALLENGES AND THE SCIENCE OF MENTAL FOCUS

Attention Strategies for quiet mental focus are more than just a way to make concentration easier. They have been effective for individuals with severe attentional challenges. The work with Sara is a good example. Sara grew up being told that she had learning disabilities. She was diagnosed with a type of Attention Deficit Disorder, along with problems in reading comprehension.

"I was always in special classes," she recalled, "where they would help me with my homework but not really teach me how to do it."

When she graduated from high school, her senior English teacher told her, "You are 18-years-old and you don't know how to write a paper. Who failed you?" Her answer was, "I guess you guys failed me, because you were supposed to teach me what to do, and obviously I don't know what to do."

In college, she practically lived in the library. While her friends were out being normal college kids, she just studied —often having to read the same page several times. "I would get to the end of a page," she lamented, "and I'd have no idea what I just read."

Writing was just as difficult. "I used to feel like I didn't know what to do, like I couldn't even write a sentence correctly. I would pull all-nighters just to write a three- or four-page paper."

Sara came to believe that learning had to be hard, because she was not really capable of understanding things. She got through college but worked harder than anyone else she knew. She got through her master's degree with the help of an editor, because she believed she was incapable of writing papers by herself.

During the first year of her PhD program, I taught Sara how to notice what her attention felt like. She discovered that the part of her that noticed things was able to notice itself, which gave her the ability to manage it. She could use visualization to make her attention spread out over a wider area of her head, or make it small in the center of her head. When she shrank her attention down into a small point, she felt how her mind snapped into focus in a way she had never been able to achieve before.

This experience was a radical shift for her, because *no one had ever taught her how to focus her mind.* Teachers told her to *focus,* and *pay attention,* but no one had taught her what to do inside of her experience to get there, in a step-by-step way. What she did instead was tighten the muscles in her body and face in an effort to force her mind to focus— which is a bit like clenching your fists to make your knees bend. Sara was using a huge amount of energy to try to focus her mind, but it wasn't effective *because she didn't know what focus felt like.*

A year later Sara reported, "I only spend a quarter of the time reading—it takes me maybe half the time to read something, and I don't have to read it twice. I read it, and I get it—I can have a conversation about it."

She had a similar improvement in her writing skills, turning out a good short paper in just a couple of hours.

"Everything comes with more ease," she said. "When I do the inner work, my mind doesn't wander." Doctoral studies are demanding, but with her newfound skills, she successfully completed her PhD studies with much less time and effort.

The Neuroscience of Focused Attention

It seems remarkable that a simple and vital process such as how to focus your attention would elude neuroscience and psychology for so long. Yet a closer look will show that the cognitive process happens in parts of the mind that receive relatively little attention in scientific research: body-felt sensation. This inner sense of one's bodily self is what Eugene Gendlin—a visionary philosopher and the creator of the Focusing process—called the *felt sense*.

Neuroscience divides this inner sense into *interoception*, the body's sense of its internal condition, and *proprioception*, the body's sense of where it is in space and how it is moving. When you walk or pick up something with your hands, those actions are guided by a sensate experience of the body's movements that is often unconscious or barely noticeable. Similarly, when you find yourself heading for the refrigerator you may or may not be aware of the actual sensations driving the desire to eat something.

Our industrialized societies value activities such as thinking and working—activities such as feeling and imagining things hold a far lower status. Barely noticeable internal senses are considered low-level feedback systems to help the brain manage the body—hardly important for directly managing brain activity. Imagining inner pictures is easily dismissed as a form of daydreaming that is unlikely to affect wellbeing other than maybe by helping people relax.

So it is hardly surprising that simple practices such as the ones shared here could hide in plain sight for so long.

In fact, until a decade ago even the brain processes that create mental focus were unknown. Two of our research team members, Dr. Lora Likova and Dr. Christopher Tyler, are pioneers in this area. Before their research, neuroscientists imagined that the mind focused attention by amping up brain signals associated with what a person was focused on. For example, if your attention was focused on one particular rose in the middle of a garden, then presumably your brain would increase the amount of energy going into creating that mental image.

However, there did not appear to be any evidence for such a process. What Drs. Likova and Tyler demonstrated was that focus works in just the opposite way—the brain reduces activation in the neurons that represent other parts of experience, so what the mind is focused on stands out.

Mental focus is commonly described using metaphors. Imagine a person standing at center stage in a darkened theater, and then suddenly a spotlight flips on and a beam of light shines down, illuminating this lone figure. That is the old idea of how mental focus works—as a spotlight of attention. Now imagine the same theater, but with all the lights on. The same person is standing in the center of the stage, but instead of a spotlight being turned on, all the lights *not* illuminating this figure are dimmed. The result is similar, but the way of getting there is quite different—and Drs. Likova and Tyler showed that this is the way the brain actually creates mental focus.

This still did not solve the question of how a person gets their brain to make those changes. When I met Drs. Likova and Tyler, I had been working on developing techniques for managing attention in a way that could create a variety of states, including mental focus. They had background in the study of attention and expertise in measuring brain activity and were interested in the study of states of consciousness. We were a perfect match.

In our first study as a team, we showed that changing your attentional stance changes your brain activity in a specific and reliable way. Each attentional stance showed a unique pattern of brain activation in at least one frequency band—frequency bands are named after Greek letters such as *alpha, beta, gamma,* and *delta.* More importantly, each time one of our participants returned to the same attentional stance, their pattern of brain activity was highly similar.

When brain activity is measured with an electro-encephalogram (EEG, for short), electrodes on the head pick up activity from the outer layer of the brain, the cortex. These patterns of brain activity are not like cans of soup arranged in neat rows with labels. They are more like wildly overgrown fields with lots of different plants jumbled together. EEG sorts these signals into different frequencies so they can be studied separately, a little like how a car radio sorts out frequencies so you can listen to just one station at a time.

The challenging part is interpreting what these signals mean in terms of the mind. Using EEG signals to detect abnormalities such as brain injury or brain tumors is easier than figuring out which signals relate to particular mental processes. For example, if you think about where your keys are three different times while wearing EEG electrodes, it is unlikely there will be any useful consistency in the results.

For this reason, it was actually surprising when we found such clear results with attentional stance. The similarity between brain signals each time an attentional stance was repeated ranged from about 50% to over 90% in the *beta* and *gamma* frequency bands (*beta* activity is usually associated with ordinary thinking activity), and positively correlated in *alpha, theta,* and *delta* (*alpha* is associated with a relaxed state, and *theta* and *delta* are more prominent during sleep).

What this means is that when you can sense where your attention is located, and you can use your imagination to move it into a specific attentional stance, you are having a direct and predictable effect on your brain's activities. An attentional stance is like a handle that gives you access to the particular package of brain activity that you need for a certain kind of task.

For example, many of our participants reported that they felt much more mentally focused when they were in a focused attentional stance in the center of the head. By now you likely have this experience as well—that *when you focus your attentional stance, you are actually focusing your mind.* This was also Sara's experience, in the story that began this chapter, and Malcolm's experience, from Chapter 4. This Attention Strategy is such a simple way to enhance a skill that most people use every day, so it is remarkable that it has not previously been described by psychology and neuroscience. Perhaps because it relies on the use of subjective inner sensation—largely ignored in these disciplines—that it has gone undiscovered for so long.

This skill of easily focusing attention is one that might be useful in every grade school along with other basic skills. It is especially important in an era where nearly every student has a cell phone. Student performance in math, reading, and science has been declining around the world since about 2010—just when portable phones and social media access became widespread. Specifically, students who spend five hours or more per day on digital media score much lower than those who spend less than an hour. While this is a serious problem that will require a variety of solutions, these advances in how to directly manage one's attention offer new tools that can be applied to help remedy this decline.

6.

JOURNEY TOWARD THE HEART

It's time for an adventure, time to leave the familiar territory of the head and venture into the part of the body below the neck. This is not just *thinking* about the body from an ordinary state of mind, or even paying more attention to the sensations of the body. The sense of "Oh, this is me," moves down into the body. It feels like "I" am down here—I am the body feeling itself.

This is an entirely different way of being—quieter, and more attuned to sensations and feeling-based intelligence. In this inner stance, insight may be present and felt in the body before it finds its way into words.

To get a sense of what this means, think of a child who is five or six years old. Little children have not yet learned to be in their heads. Their attention is still in the whole body—as they play, their movements and their voices come from the whole body. Their experience of the world in this whole-body attentional stance is not just a less-developed form of adult experience, it is of an entirely different quality as well. There is an aliveness to the world, an intensity to imagination, and a magic just waiting to be discovered.

When I was four years old, I had a grey-and-white sock monkey. I loved that sock monkey and wanted to carry it with me everywhere I went. When I looked at the monkey, it felt alive just the way another person was alive. Using my adult words to describe what I remember from that age, there was a sense of intimate connection with the monkey. I did not have brothers or sisters but having this monkey was like having someone to be with, even when no one else was around.

At some point, the monkey ended up stored in a box, When I was about eight years old, I discovered it again. I pulled it out, eager to feel the old connection, but the magic was gone. The sock monkey no longer felt like a companion —it was just an object. I remember feeling some sadness at the shift and also realizing that this was part of growing up. I put the monkey back into the box where I had found it.

Leaving the magic of childhood behind is a necessary process for gaining the mental skills needed to be an adult. But recovering access to the rest of the body is part of what restores magic and aliveness, and what adds back creativity and intuition, once the limits of intellectual smartness are discovered. This recovery of the body is not an instantaneous one; it is a process of re-awakening the body by bringing attention—one's sense of "I"—down from the head and practicing being oneself from the heart, the belly, and the core.

Before you engage this next step, I suggest you practice bringing yourself to a focused attentional stance in the center of your head several times a day for three or four days. When you feel comfortable with the process, here is a next step:

MOVE YOUR ATTENTION (FIGURE 6.1)

The first step is a small, easy one. Bring yourself to a focused attentional stance in the center of the head, using whichever method is easiest for you. Become the sensation or the point of light in the center of the head that draws and releases each breath, that receives each sound, that notices each sensation of your body.

Now allow yourself to ease downward about an inch (2–3 cm), so that you are behind the center of your face instead of behind your eyes. If part of you is watching yourself go "down there," invite that part to ease downward as well, so you feel that you are "down here," behind the center of your face.

You may notice that your vision becomes slightly softer, and that body sensations become a little more obvious. It may feel natural to hold your gaze slightly downward.

Figure 6.1

This first small movement is just enough for you to feel that your attention—your felt sense of "I"—can move from one place to another. Later exercises will help you bring it down to the chest, the low belly, and beyond. For now, notice that when the source of your attention moves, even just an inch, or a few centimeters, it subtly changes your state of mind. When you move it farther, and remain longer, the impact on your state of consciousness will increase.

Moving attention is like moving the body: you do it by feel. When an infant lies on her back and watches this thing that she will later call her hand, she sees that it shows up at odd times and moves back and forth, apparently of its own volition. Perhaps later, the baby will notice that she feels certain body sensations every time the hand-thing moves. Through these sensations she will learn to control the hand, and keep track of where it is.

Try it for yourself with this simple exercise.

TRACK YOUR HAND

After you read these instructions, stop for a moment and place one hand behind your back. Then close your eyes, count slowly to ten, and ask yourself whether your hand is still behind your back. How do you know whether it is still there?

Without opening your eyes, move your hand out from behind your back. Notice what it *feels like* to move your hand, and to be aware of feeling its movement. Then open your eyes.

Of course, you can track where your hand is because you can feel where it is: a subtle sensation, a sort of *here-is-my-hand* sensation, is behind your *here-is-my-back* sensation. The intention to move the hand is really an intention to move the *here-is-my-hand* sensation. Yet those sensations are so familiar, so present in every waking moment, that it takes a pause, and a little effort, to actually notice them.

Noticing where attention sits, and learning to move it, is just the same: it means finding your *here-is-my-attention* sensation—and noticing, "Oh, this is *me*, right here"—then noticing that you can move that sensation to a different location, much in the way you can move your *here-is-my-hand* sensation.

But enough of words and ideas and preliminaries. Come along on the next steps of the journey, and find out for yourself what it is like to change your attentional stance in a more profound way.

In the exercises introduced in this chapter and throughout the following chapters, you will be guided to bring your attention down into the chest and abdomen, rather than staying in the head. The normal tendency is to sit in the head while reading, which may interfere with the process you are learning. Try reading through the exercise, getting a clear sense of what the steps are, and see if you can move through the practice without reading.

These exercises can be done with eyes open or closed, though sometimes the effort needed to keep the eyes closed can keep some of your attention in the face area. Often it helps to allow the eyes to be partly open, and relaxed with a soft gaze that is receptive rather than looking at anything in particular.

JOURNEY TOWARD THE HEART

Touch lightly on the top of the head, then lift your finger away and notice the sensation that stays on your head. Imagine it sitting like a little point of light on the top of your head. Imagine you can feel it drifting slowly downward, until it comes to rest in the center of your head, behind your gently closed eyes.

Now imagine you are this sensation or point of light. Feel yourself as the point that inhales your breath, and releases it again. Imagine the sounds around you and the sensations in your body are arriving here, where you are in the center of your head.

As you breathe, imagine that the air you inhale is coming right to where you are in the center of the head, strengthening the sensation or brightening the light the way an ember brightens when you blow on it.

Allow yourself to ease downward about an inch (2–3 cm). Feel yourself sitting behind the center of your face instead of behind the eyes. If part of you is still watching the point of light go "down there," invite that part of you to let go so that it is "down here" behind the center of your face.

Now let go, and allow yourself to drift down to the back of your throat. Be the sensation or point of light that allows itself to slide down the back of the throat, through the neck.

Let yourself ease down into the chest, deep in along the front of your spine, until you come to the center of the chest.

If you have difficulty moving through the throat area, just come as far down as you can—it is enough. The fact that you are noticing some obstacle to your downward movement is clear evidence that you are able to move your attention. Notice this success, and appreciate it.

Whether you are still somewhere in the throat or you have made it all the way down to the center of the chest, notice the sounds around you, and be the sensation or the point of light that receives the sounds here, right where you are. As you breathe, be the point of light that draws and releases each breath, imagining you can feel the air arriving right where you are. Be the sensation or point of light that gently notices the sensations of your body.

It is quite usual for beginners in the process of moving their attention down from the head to feel as if there is something "in the way" of moving through the throat, as if some obstacle in the felt space of the body blocks their way. Chapter 8 will explain what these are, and how to deal with them. For now, this next exercise will allow you to bypass the throat and move directly to the heart.

LOCATE THE HEART (FRONT OF CHEST) (FIG. 6.2)

Take one finger and touch lightly at the center of your chest, then lift the finger away. Notice the gentle sensation that remains at the center of your chest after you lift your finger. Imagine that sensation as a point of light, poised on your skin, if the image is helpful. Imagine that this sensation or point of light slides slightly back into your chest, until it is just below the skin. Imagine that you are this point of light in the front of your chest.

Notice each of the sounds around you, and imagine these sounds are arriving here, at the front of the chest. Feel yourself as the sensation or point of light in the chest that receives the sounds. Imagine that as this point, you draw in each breath to where you are, right through the chest and the upper back, and then release it again.

If you notice that part of you is watching from your head or your face, invite that part to melt and slide down to where you are at the front of your chest, so you feel yourself "*down here*" in the chest. With each breath, imagine that this sensation or point of light becomes stronger, warmer, more comfortable.

Give yourself permission to savor the rich silence for a few moments before you open your eyes.

Figure 6.2

This may be a familiar place that you have touched at moments in the past, without knowing how you got here or how to find your way back. For others, this may feel like a wholly different experience.

When attention sits focused in the body—not focused *on* the body, but *in* the body—the mind is quiet, released from many of the inner conversations, judgments, and worries that happen in the head, in the thinking mind. This too is the mind, here at the heart.

As thoughts slow in the quietly focused mind, perception sharpens, and a different kind of knowing comes forward. The experience of one's own mind becomes less about words and pictures, and more about sensations in a spacious sense of self—sensations that give cues about what the mind is doing, and what is happening in the experience of the people around you.

This state of experiencing the mind *in* the body is often called embodiment. *This is not about being in your head and feeling your body, and it is not about the fact that the brain is connected to the whole body. It is about a shifted state of consciousness, a game-changing state of mind.*

Whether you want to cultivate better bounce-back from stress, more felt connection with others, stronger presence in groups, or a dozen other skills that use presence or relies on shifting your way of being with others, the practice of bringing your attention down into your body opens the doors to a new, different, and powerful way of being yourself in the world.

7.

ENTER THE HEART

As you grow the heart's ability to feel, this capacity becomes a strength rather than a weakness. *Courage* comes from the French word *coeur*, for *heart*—so to "take courage" and "take heart" are the same thing. The head is clever and strategic, but it is the heart that is brave, wise, and effective in ways that the ordinary mind can never match.

Cesar, a consultant and advisor, wanted to be more embodied. He already knew how to bring himself down into his body, but he could not feel the back of his body, and he did not feel like he was fully present in his heart. I invited him to find the space that was his heart and ask that space what it needed to be present. The answer was "Willingness" —his willingness to be present in his heart. Cesar was not sure he wanted to be that vulnerable.

Cesar's belief is a common one —that if you show up with your heart, you are more vulnerable. But avoiding vulnerability by sidestepping the heart is like trying to avoid disease by killing germs. There is not enough hand sanitizer and mouthwash to kill off all of the organisms each human being encounters on a daily basis, no matter how fastidiously hygienic they might be—and most of the time, most of us do not get ill. Keeping reasonably clean is important, of course, but a healthy immune system keeps the body healthy by being more powerful than organisms that try to invade.

When losses or disappointments happen, the heart will feel the hurt. But when the heart is filled with your presence—when your attention is located in your heart—it is better at bearing pain, and more able to bounce back.

Cesar chose to be willing to be fully in his heart.

The previous exercise brought attention to the area of the heart but kept the sensation at the surface of the chest. In order to fully activate the heart's intelligence it is necessary to expand the attention back toward the center of the body at the level of the heart, as in this next exercise.

After reading through the exercise, and getting a good sense of the process, put the book aside and try it with eyes closed, or gently open with soft focus.

DEEPENING INTO THE HEART (FIG. 7.1)

Take one finger and touch gently on the sternum at the center of the chest, then lift the finger away. Notice the sensation that stays on the skin after you lift your finger. Imagine that sensation as a point of light, poised on the skin, if an image feels useful.

Imagine that this sensation or point of light slowly expands backwards a couple of inches (6–8 cm), all the way to the front of your spine. Imagine that this little ball of sensation or glowing light fills the space from the center of your body to the front of your chest.

Feel yourself as this small glowing area extending deep into the center of your chest. Notice each of the sounds around you, and imagine you can feel these sounds as they arrive here, right where you are. Feel yourself as a glow in the chest that receives each sound.

Imagine you draw the breath in through the wall of the chest and through the upper back—that each breath comes directly into the body, to where you are in the chest. Feel the air as you draw it in and release it.

Invite any part of your attention that is still in your head or your face to soften and slide down here, down into the center of the chest, so you feel that your attention is coming from "*down here*" in the center of the chest, rather than from "*down there*" in the chest.

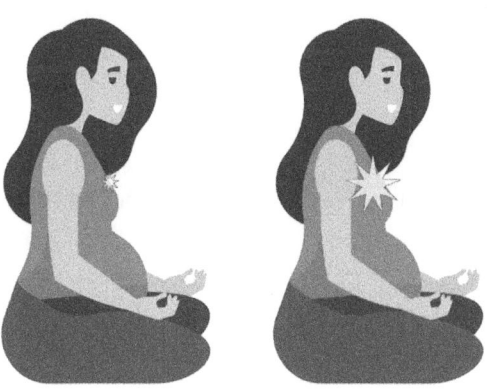

Figure 7.1

The focused intelligence of the heart is attuned to feeling, but it is not sentimental. When attention sits centered in the chest, it can bring a new and different kind of information, a *felt intelligence*. This intelligence is not just about feelings. It is also a feeling-based intelligence: insight that is present and felt in the body before it finds its way into words.

Teisha was in a new job at a small company and was not feeling landed. She was achieving her work goals but did not feel lined up with her co-workers or her boss. She had been practicing being more in her body during work, which helped her feel more at ease. But she was distracted out of her relaxed state whenever a co-worker spoke to her. She wanted to know how to stay in her body when she was around other people at work.

I practiced speaking with Teisha the way her co-workers did and asked her to listen in her normal way. She noticed that my words pulled her back into her head and into a distracted state of mind. Then I asked her to imagine that my voice was arriving at the center of her chest rather than at her ears. As she did this, she noticed a significant shift in her experience of me. Instead of being distracted by my words, she stayed quiet internally. As she listened quietly, she could feel she had an answer for me even before she had actual words.

Something clicked for Teisha. She realized that she already did this when she worked with numbers. As she described it, "I can look at a spreadsheet, and I have a feeling of where I need to look. I'm usually able to zero in pretty quickly on any problem areas." When she read words, she repeated them in her head—as most people do—but when she read numbers, she just *took them in* without repeating them. This gave her a *felt sense* of where to look for problems.

Teisha noted that her boss was always able to listen to others and come up with just the right question. She recognized that she could learn to do the same by taking a skill she already had with numbers and applying it in a new way, as a listening skill. She recognized that this would keep her present in her body so she could be quieter and more focused, and a better listener. With this skill, Teisha reported that she was much more comfortable in her work environment.

Her company noticed the change as well, and within a few months she received a promotion. But this was no more than external validation of a change she had already made within herself.

Finding Flow

Presence in the heart can contribute to many aspects of life besides work. One of these is exercise. If you have experienced a peak or flow state during exercise, you know how exhilarating it is—how it feels like the world is flowing through you. Physical activity becomes nearly effortless as the minutes or miles fly by. Experienced athletes know the value and pleasure of a flow state, but typically have no control over when a flow experience will kick in.

The body map of Attention Strategies changes this. My introduction to the flow state was in guiding Marlis Marolt-Sender—now Dr. Marolt-Sender—in her doctoral research. Marlis herself is a remarkable athlete, the daughter of an Olympic alpine skier. I showed Marlis how attentional stance gave rapid access to high-level states, and she immediately wanted to research the attentional stance of flow.

The psychological interpretation of flow makes it sound like something you do with your ordinary thinking mind, but it is much more and much different than that. Flow is a thoroughgoing shift in state of consciousness that affects the whole body. Marlis wanted to measure the attentional stance of flow.

For her doctoral dissertation, Marlis recruited 28 endurance athletes—high-performing athletes at the national and international competition level. Some were runners, some also participated in other events, such as swimming, bicycling, or triathlons. She asked each one to recall a flow experience in vivid detail, including how it felt in the body. Then she asked them to draw a picture that represented this experience and would help bring them back to it.

I flew in and met with Marlis and her participants, and led a training on how to recognize one's attentional stance. During this event, participants were asked to indicate where their attention was located after reading a news story, and after recalling their experience in a flow state, prompted by the drawing they had made.

To no one's surprise, these athletes reported that after reading a news story, their attention was located in their heads. When they recalled their flow experience, however, their attentional stance was entirely different. Each athlete indicated the location of their attention on outlines of the body, and these drawings showed that the attentional stance of flow is located in the area of the heart.

During a break in the training session, one of the athletes was overheard saying that he realized he would no longer need to wait for the flow state to show up, *he could just go there.* This is, of course, the benefit of mapping attentional stances on the body—high-performance states can be directly accessed using an Attention Strategy.

Even if you are not an Olympic athlete, flow can make your exercise session much more pleasant. This builds on the previous exercise where you expand back into the front of the chest, then use your imagination to call in an inspiring image—not in your head, but in the space you imagine in front of you.

HEART FLOW (FIG. 7.2)

Touch gently on the center of the chest, then lift the finger away. Notice the sensation that remains on the skin after you lift the finger. Feel the sensation, and if an image helps, imagine it as a point of light right on the front of your sternum.

Imagine that this sensation or point of light slowly expands backwards a couple of inches, (5–8 cm), all the way to the front of your spine. Imagine that this little ball of sensation or glowing light fills the space from the center of your body to the front of your chest.

In the open space in front of your chest, call in an image of something that inspires you, and feel for the quality of uplift, of inspiration, right here where you are seated in the chest.

Be this warmth or stirring in the chest that feels itself, that takes in the beauty, the elegance, whatever it is that moves your heart. Feel these sensations strengthen a little with each breath. If the feelings begin to lift up and out of the chest, draw them back. Give them room to expand, yet keep them rooted here, close to you.

Figure 7.2

Practice igniting the flow state, then enter this state when you are about to exercise. This is also a state you can use when you have a long meeting or work project that requires endurance. With a flow state, you can directly generate positive sensations in your body, without the need for a story in your mind that makes you feel good about yourself or about life. The positive feelings of flow aren't about anything—they just are, regardless of what is going on around you.

Healing with Gratitude

Another area to apply attentional stance in the heart is gratitude practice. Gratitude can increase wellbeing, but writing daily lists of things you are grateful doesn't always work—and if you don't feel better there's the risk of feeling like a gratitude failure.

Gratitude practices are much more reliably effective when you do them from an attentional stance in the heart. They are much less reliable when done from an attentional stance in the head, because gratitude is a body-felt sensation, not a thought.

If your gratitude practice isn't working, or you would like to see what the benefits are, give this one a try:

GRATITUDE YOU CAN FEEL (FIG. 7.3)

Bring yourself into the heart flow state, using the first two paragraphs of the previous exercise.

In the space in front of your chest, call up a vivid image of something that you are grateful for. As you connect with this image, imagine that you are going to feel a gentle spreading sensation of warmth where you are, here in the chest. As the warmth begins, imagine that with each breath, it becomes warmer and more radiant with each inhale, and that it spreads just a little more with each exhale.

Be the center of the chest that feels itself, that contemplates the image of what awakens gratitude, and that feels this spreading warmth within it. Bask in the warmth.

As you have small quiet moments through the day, remember this feeling and call it back to you.

Figure 7.3

Whichever heart-based practice you use, remember that entering the heart with one's attention is quite different than sitting in the head and feeling the heart from there. Down here, in the center of the chest, what the heart knows and what it feels can be noticed quietly, without interference from the usual stories that are rehearsed over and over by the part of the mind that sits in the head.

Endlessly repeated storylines happen in the body as well, as you will discover in the next chapter. These can be relieved in a different way.

8.

INTEGRATION

In an earlier chapter, I noted that people often encounter obstacles when trying to move their attention through the throat area. It can feel as if there is an invisible barrier that blocks the way. Imagine you were walking blindfolded down a hallway, a hand on one wall to keep you oriented, and you ran into a big beachball that you had to squeeze around, or that blocked your way completely. Meeting one of these obstacles in the body is a bit like that.

If your goal is to get to a particular attentional stance, you can often just go around the obstacle or, as with getting from the head to the heart, restart the process with a sensation that is closer to your goal. But sometimes the barrier is right where you want to go. For example, you might be able to sit in the attentional stance near the front of the chest, but when you try to deepen into the heart area, you run into a block. Or you might be able to feel yourself at the top of your head, but a barrier keeps you from dropping down into the middle of the head.

The good news is that when you find one of these obstacles, it is an opportunity to resolve an unintegrated part of yourself. You may have heard about emotions or traumas from the past being stored "in the body." These obstacles are places where those stories and feelings from the past live. Of course, they are not literally sitting in the head or chest or throat—a surgeon would not find anything if they looked inside your body. Nor are they just stories and feelings. These blockages represent aspects of yourself that are trying to protect you from events that happened in the past.

The ways they work to protect you vary. Often they create some kind of an emotional reaction—fear, irritation, anxiety, impatience. Ha-joon, a business executive, shared that when he was in a grocery store the previous week, the clerk said something that just hit him the wrong way, and the next thing he knew, he was ranting at the clerk. He said, "It was like I was just watching myself, and I couldn't really stop myself or do anything about it."

When one of these protective parts is triggered, it can sort of hijack you, take over your behavior, and convince you that your reaction is justified. There's an expression that someone "pushed your buttons." In the language of that metaphor, these protective parts are the buttons that get pushed.

In my research on how to help these fragmented parts of the inner self resolve, conducted with a colleague, Dr. Genine Smith, we have referred to these as *dissociated ego states*. It is well known in some approaches such as analytical psychology that these aspects of the self seem to have their own agenda and their own sense of agency. It's kind of like having a part of your personality that has a mind of its own and does its own thing.

In the Attention Strategies model, these younger parts of the self can usually be experienced in a particular location in the body—they have a *location* on the body map. Particular types of inner parts tend to be experienced in certain areas of the body. For example, parts that are perfectionistic or always scanning to make sure everything gets done are often located near the front of the head. Parts that have to do with issues related to expressing thoughts or feelings are more likely to be in the throat. Parts related to relationship issues are often in the heart or chest area, and difficult events from childhood are often experienced in the stomach or belly.

Most people have difficult experiences of some kind in childhood—an injury or severe illness; losing a parent, a sibling, or a grandparent; feeling rejection or ridicule or physical aggression from a family member, playmate, or classmate. Even ordinary life experiences can be traumatic: moving to a different town or city, being teased by an older sibling, being embarrassed in front of friends or classmates at school. Trauma does not have to be something exceptional; it can also be the impact of commonplace experiences in which the person felt powerless.

Here is an example of how Ingrid experienced one of these blockages, and how it was resolved.

Ingrid, a graduate student studying to become a psychotherapist, shared that with the Attention Strategies techniques she was able to be more relaxed about her meditation practice. The step-by-step understanding allowed her to feel like she had control over the process—without which her anxiety would come up.

This wording caught my attention. It sounded like some part of her inner self was always trying to scan her life to make sure everything was in control and getting done correctly. I described this and asked her whether she would like to try to discover where this part of herself was located, and she said, "Oh, it's definitely more in my head. That's the perfectionist part of me. It's when I'm in my head that I'm very critical of myself."

I asked Ingrid to bring herself into the attentional stance of focus in the center of her head, behind where she felt this part of herself. I invited her to imagine she could see this part that criticized her, sitting up in the front part of her head. Once she could imagine it there, I suggested that she ask it if it would be willing to let go of whatever it was trying to do for her.

"It's hesitant," she said. "It's hesitant because this is what keeps me on top of everything." Of course, this part was in fact doing that important job for her. I prompted her to ask the part how old she was when it started helping her in this way. She squeezed her eyes shut as tears began to form, and she exclaimed, "Wow, wow, wow, wow." I encouraged her to let the feelings come.

After a few moments she said, "A vision of me came up right away. I was maybe in the fourth grade, and there was a math problem—a math test—that I didn't understand. And I didn't have anyone around to help me. And at school, the teacher told me she would keep me at the school until I finished the test. I wouldn't be able to go home until then." She sobbed. "And everybody had gone home, and I was the only one left. And it was getting dark. And I was so upset, because it wasn't that I didn't want to do it, I just couldn't understand it." After a few more tears, Ingrid said, "Wow, wow, wow, wow, that was the vision that immediately came to me when you asked me that question."

From this we figured out that she must have been about ten or eleven years old at the time of this event. I suggested that Ingrid ask this part of herself whether she wanted to keep holding the responsibility of trying to make sure everything was taken care of, so this kind of shaming experience would never happen again. Now that Ingrid was grown up, would this young part like to let go of this heavy responsibility and be taken care of by the adult part of Ingrid?

After a long pause, and speaking from the perspective of her younger self, Ingrid said, "Yes, yes, I'm definitely ready to release that." I asked Ingrid to show this young part of herself what she looked like now as an adult and assure her that, as an adult, she would be able to take care of things just fine. The young part could just relax and release the responsibility back to the adult self. I encouraged Ingrid to acknowledge that this young part had worked hard, and suggested she might want to let her younger self know how grateful she was for the loyal support and the efforts to make sure that everything was okay.

Ingrid said she saw her younger self plopping down on a sofa with huge relief, as if saying, "Finally I don't have to hold this responsibility any more." Ingrid focused internally for a few moments, then said, "She's showing me the way I've re-invented my life several times, successfully, and that I am in control now."

From this it was clear that this younger self was actually aware of events in Ingrid's life—often these inner parts are only dimly aware of the person's outer life—yet she continued in her responsibilities because she had not been given permission to let go of it. Ingrid noted that "that's why she was hesitant to give up the role."

Ingrid opened her eyes. She looked radiant. "Wow. The pressure that I had on my head is no longer there!" I encouraged Ingrid to ask this younger part if it would like to come home and be part of her again. "Yes, yes, she very much wants to come home." As she held this invitation, Ingrid was grinning widely. "So much joy, so much joy to be integrated."

As Ingrid's experience illustrates, even one occasion of harsh discipline in childhood can result in a dissociated ego state that, unless resolved, may create psychological stress, hypervigilance, and compulsive achievement well into adulthood.

While working with Ingrid's inner part required an experienced facilitator, sometimes they resolve more easily. Marco was an Attention Strategies workshop participant who was trying to focus his attention in the center of his head by touching the top of his head and moving the sensation downward. He reported that "it is like I am on a trampoline—I can go down a little ways but then I get pushed back up."

I asked Marco to begin by touching the back of his head instead. By creating a sensation on the part of the head that extends backward just above the neck, and then moving that sensation forward, he was able to focus his attention in the center of his head behind his eyes. I asked Marco to imagine that he could look up from this location and see the part at the top of his head that blocked him when he tried to bring the sensation down into his head. He took a moment, then said, "Yes, I can see it."

"What does it look like when you imagine it?" I asked.

"It is like a dark, grey pancake shape," he replied. I suggested he ask it whether it was ready to let go of the responsibilities it was holding for him. "Yes, yes it is." I encouraged Marco to tell this part of himself that it could just relax and let go, that everything was fine, and he felt it soften. Then I suggested he ask it whether it would like to come back and be part of him again. He reported that it was very happy to do this. He felt a warmth in the center of his chest as the distance between himself and this protective part closed.

Notice that in this case, there was no need for an extended dialogue or negotiation. He did not need to find out how this part of himself saw its role, what age it became active, or anything about the events that triggered its separation from his central self. This protective part was ready to release its tasks and resolve back into the adult Marco in response to a simple invitation.

Here is an exercise you can try when you encounter an area in your body map that will not let you enter. Sometimes the process is simple, as in Marco's case, and sometimes you may need to find a coach or therapist who can work with you when the process is more complex. Keep in mind that just by finding where this part of yourself lives in your experience—just by locating it on your body map—you have made an important discovery.

DIALOGUE WITH A PART OF YOUR INNER SELF (FIG. 8.1)

When you encounter an area in the felt space of the body that your attention cannot enter, use your imagination to pretend you can see it, and notice how big it is, how far it extends in each direction, what shape and color it is.

Bring yourself into a focused attentional stance—in the center of your head if the part is in the head, in your heart if it is in the chest or throat.

Imagine you can have a conversation with it, and ask it if it is ready to let go of the responsibilities it holds for you. See if a response comes to you in the form of words that form in your mind. Notice whether it tightens and draws back, or softens towards you.

If it resists, either in the words you hear or the tightening you feel, let it know that everything is alright now. You are now a grown-up, you can handle what it is trying to do for you, and it is okay for it to relax and release its responsibilities back to you.

When it relents and softens, imagine that you receive the resources it has been holding for you, as if they are flowing into the center of your chest.

When you sense that the flow has stopped, ask this part of yourself whether it would like to come home and be part of you again. If it is willing, invite it to return to your heart.

Figure 8.1

This process is not like psychotherapy, because it works directly with sensations in your body, and uses imagination to invite these inner areas of tension to relax. Dialoguing with many of these inner parts may briefly reference memories of simple disappointments or stresses from the past, but in this approach there is no need to understand or work through those past experiences, so there is often no need for the expertise of a mental health professional.

However, if you know you have trauma in your history, or if you sense that there may be a connection to trauma associated with the sensations—or absence of sensations—in some part of your body, make sure you are also working with a psychotherapist who has experience with recovery from trauma.

In my experience as a university educator and coach for business leaders, resolving these inner aspects of your self is one of the most powerful tools for personal growth, and for getting past old feelings and habits that no longer serve. This topic deserves a book of its own, but now you have a glimpse of how to understand and engage with one of the challenges you may encounter as you create a body map of your own inner self.

As these aspects of self resolve into your central self, the felt space inside of your body will become easier to navigate.

9.

FIND MINDFUL CONTENTMENT IN THE BELLY

Happiness is not something you find "out there" with what you can buy or eat or watch, or who you can hang out with. It is something you generate in your own body. People say that happiness is within, but lots of other experiences are also available "within." In my within-space I can easily find anxiety, worry, and dread, to name just a few—so "going within" isn't specific enough.

Happiness is something you create by using a specific attentional stance—sitting in the space of the belly. Here, as you use your body's imagination, you invite in the qualities of warmth and contentment until your abdomen is glowing with quiet satisfaction. You become the belly that feels itself, that receives the sounds and sensations, that draws and releases each breath. In this state, time slows down. There are no worries. In fact, there are few thoughts of any sort. If life challenges do come to mind, the sensations here send your nervous system the message that things are okay.

Bringing yourself down to the belly is as simple as any other attentional stance. Before trying the exercise, it may be helpful to understand a little of what science has learned about positive emotions. There are two distinctly different kinds of positive emotion: excited ones and relaxed ones. People looking for happiness are usually trying to work up the excited ones, but it is the relaxed ones that come closer to real happiness.

In neuroscience language the excited ones are called *high-arousal positive affect* (HAPA). Arousal is about the electrical state of neurons, not about readiness for sex. These high-arousal positive affect states include joy, excitement, surprise, inspiration, and enthusiasm. Calm, relaxed, and contented positive states—or *low-arousal positive affect states*, abbreviated as LAPA—include gratitude, awe, serenity, contentment.

Early findings in this relatively new area of research show that the contented LAPA states are much more effective at countering stress, anxiety, and depression than the exciting HAPA states. Of course, HAPA states are great fun—without them life gets a bit dull. But HAPA emotions typically can't be sustained for very long—and these high-arousal states show *no association with life satisfaction*. LAPA states, by contrast, are connected with life satisfaction, something that seems just a little closer to real happiness than short bursts of thrilling feelings.

Mindfulness

LAPA states are also associated with mindfulness. These days, the term *mindfulness* is everywhere. There is a version where instead of just thinking, you notice that you're thinking. This has the fancy name of *metacognition*. Useful, sure, but hardly a game-changer. There's another version in which you decide to intentionally accept the circumstances in your life, and commit yourself to making new choices based on your values. Who could complain about that? But neither of these sounds remotely like the peaceful contented state that you see expressed on the face of a Buddha statue.

How does one get to this other kind of mindfulness, the one that is supposed to feel really good, and make you peaceful and contented inside? If you lived somewhere in Asia a hundred years ago and you wanted to learn mindfulness, you couldn't just pop down to a class on Tuesday nights to learn it. Maybe you could get some helpful hints from a passing monk, but mastering it required a much bigger commitment.

Someone who wanted to learn mindfulness in a thorough way would need to leave their home, their family, their fields or business, and move to a monastery or monastic village built around a Buddhist teacher of mindfulness or *vipassana*. There they would live and eat and work and study, taking it in as much from the tone and atmosphere of the community as from the specific teachings. They might spend years, dedicating the rest of their life.

Dropping out of ordinary life is not a good option for most modern people who would like to benefit from mindfulness—and not everyone wants to join a religion. But the way mindfulness is taught now has not advanced much from the early traditional contexts—except that instead of being immersed in a community of practice, there is often just personal practice for some minutes a day, or a weekly class to attend. The challenge is how to master the state of mindfulness without day-and-night immersion in a community of practice.

This is where neuroscience can help. If an attentional stance can be identified that creates low-arousal positive affect—a LAPA state—and this state also corresponds with traditional descriptions of mindfulness, then an Attention Strategy should be able to bring you into mindfulness quickly and reliably. No special beliefs are needed. The speed and efficiency of an Attention Strategy balances out the fact that people today have much less time to learn meditation or practice mindfulness with others.

Working with my colleagues Drs. Lora Likova and Christopher Tyler, we tested a variety of attentional stances and found just one that fit with the traditional descriptions of vipassana, and also generated a LAPA state—the stance of Mindful Contentment. Naturally, this is not a Buddhist state, because it is being offered in the context of psychology. Only practices in the context of teachings that include the Buddhist eightfold path could lead to a Buddhist state. But from the perspective of psychology, the attentional stance of Mindful Contentment seems to be a close match for the mental state generated by vipassana practice in Buddhist communities.

It's great to have an idea that, in theory, checks all the boxes. But it needs to be tested to see if it really works. There are lots of ideas that look great on paper but don't work in real life. In recent months, we have been running a small study with meditation novices to see whether using this stance would reduce stress and increase mindfulness. Even though the study is not published as of this writing, I can share with you our results so far.

Each of our 15 participants, all beginners, received about 30 minutes of instruction on how to enter the attentional stance of Mindful Contentment. After this short introduction and practice with a 10-minute recording, these participants experienced a 69% *reduction in stress* and a 72% *increase in mindfulness*—both results with strong statistical significance. (Statistics can tell you how likely it is that your results came about by chance, so "strong significance" means there is only a tiny probability that the results are a fluke.) Mindfulness typically takes weeks or months to learn effectively, but by learning the Attention Strategy for this state, these participants were able to gain real benefits in stress reduction and increased mindfulness in less than an hour of instruction and practice. In a second study with experienced mindfulness meditators, we found that using the attentional stance created with the Mindful Contentment exercise was more effective at reducing stress than a stance in the chest, regardless of whether participants were doing their own meditation practice or using the Attention Strategy.

Of course, research is a complicated process, and strong results are rare, but our study achieved very positive results, gained in a remarkably short time. They are enough for us to conclude that the attentional stance located in the space of the belly is a powerful way to generate a LAPA state—one that creates positive emotions, life satisfaction, and mindfulness. We can also say that it seems quite similar in its effect to the core Buddhist practice of vipassana.

Here is the practice, which begins with the Heart Flow state, then adds the "Gratitude You Can Feel" exercise, and from there moves down into the belly:

MINDFUL CONTENTMENT (FIG. 9.1)

Heart Flow
Touch gently on the center of the chest, then lift the finger away. Notice the sensation that remains on the skin after you lift the finger. Feel the sensation and if an image helps, imagine it as a point of light right on the sternum.

Imagine that this sensation or point of light slowly expands backwards several inches (6–8 cm) until it touches the front of your spine. Imagine that this little a ball of sensation or glowing light fills the space from the center of your body to the front of your chest.

Feel yourself as the area in the center and front of the chest that receives each sound, that draws and releases each breath.

Gratitude You Can Feel

In the space in front of your heart, call up a vivid image of something that you are grateful for. As you connect with this image, imagine that you are going to feel a gentle spreading sensation of warmth where you are here in the chest. As the warmth begins, imagine that with each breath, it becomes warmer and more radiant with each inhale, and that it spreads just a little more with each exhale.

Be the center of the chest that feels itself, that contemplates the image which awakens gratitude, and that feels this spreading warmth within it. Bask in the warmth.

Enter the Belly

Imagine that this spreading warmth is like a spring bubbling up in the center of your chest. Now imagine that it begins to flow down the front of your spine, down between the lungs, behind the stomach, down into the space of the belly.

Imagine that this flow of warm gratitude begins to fill the space of the belly, beginning from the bottom. Feel it as it fills the space of the belly, first up to the level of the navel, then all the way up to the stomach.

Now imagine that you can move into this flow of gratitude and flow down with it, down the front of the spine, all the way to the space of the belly. Allow yourself to become the space of the belly.

Notice the sounds around you, and receive them here, in the belly. Be the belly that feels itself, that draws each breath right in through the wall of the belly and through the low back. Be the belly that feels itself and that notices the sensations of the body—the pelvis and legs below, the chest and head above.

With each breath, imagine that the warmth of the belly begins to glow just a little brighter, until the radiance from the warmth shines out into the space in front of the belly and glows behind the back.

Be the belly that feels itself, that receives the sounds and the sensations of the body, that draws and releases each breath, and that radiates its warmth into the space around the body. Be the belly that feels contentment.

Welcome to a new way to be yourself in your body. This place of peace, of quiet contentment, is one you can learn to carry into your daily life. It can reduce your stress, increase your ability to pay careful attention, and enhance your relationships.

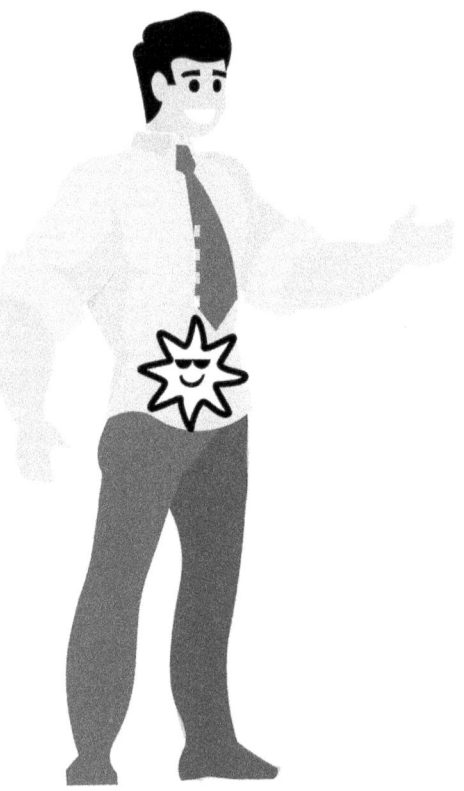

Figure 9.1

10.

THE WHOLE-BODY BRAIN

Now you have had an experience of how "you," as your attention, can be located in places other than your head. How is this possible, when the brain is the seat of consciousness, and it is located in the head? What if mind extends through the whole body as well? The brain is considered the organ of consciousness, but what if brain-like processes are happening throughout the body? Maybe the sentience and intelligence of the organism is located not just in the brain, but in the whole body. This chapter will provide some context and evidence for what is an upending of conventional ideas about where mind is located.

A little more than a hundred years ago, scientists thought of neurons in the brain as a complex electrical grid. Imagine a network of Christmas lights winking on and off, sending signals to each other by means of wires. Early ideas about the brain were something like this.

Then a Spanish neuroscientist, Santiago Ramón y Cajal, used newly-developed methods of staining brain tissue, and looked carefully at the structure of neurons. He found there was a gap between where the "wires" from one neuron ended, and where another neuron started—what came to be called the *synaptic gap*. This was big news. It would be like discovering that the lights on your Christmas tree worked together, even though the wires from each light bulb did not quite connect with the next bulb. It was a discovery that won him a Nobel prize in 1906.

Soon afterwards, other neuroscientists discovered that neurons communicated with each other across these gaps by means of chemical signals, rather than electrical signals. These chemicals were called *neurotransmitters*, because they help transmit information between neurons. For many years, neurotransmitters were commonly referred to as *brain chemicals*, because it was assumed they only occurred in the brain, as part of the process of creating the mind.

Exactly how neurotransmitters relayed signals from one neuron to another in humans brains was not clearly understood until the early 1970s, when Candace Pert and Solomon Snyder showed that molecules of these neurotransmitters could bind to *receptors* in other neurons, much the same way a key fits into a lock. When you put a key into the ignition in a car and turn it, the engine starts. In a similar way, when a chemical key emitted by one neuron connects with the right kind of keyhole in another neuron, it "turns on" something in that neuron's functions.

The first receptor that Pert and Snyder found was for opiates—that is, a receptor for drugs like morphine and heroin. This was not evidence that humans were designed to use heroin. Instead, it suggested that drugs such as morphine relieve pain because they mimic morphine-like substances the body already produces—protein-like molecules that came to be called *endorphins*.

While this discovery of endorphin receptors was groundbreaking, in the following decades Pert and her team found something even more revolutionary. Because these receptors had to do with controlling pain, they looked for them not just in the brain, but in the rest of the body as well. It turned out these receptors, as well as those for every other neurotransmitter, were found in many parts of the body—not just the brain.

This means that very sorts of chemicals that were supposedly unique to brain activity—the activity that helps the brain create the mind—are at work in locations *throughout the body*, including major nerve centers along the spine, the heart, the kidneys, the digestive tract, the endocrine glands and reproductive organs, and the lymphatic system. *The neurotransmitters once known as brain chemicals are everywhere in the body.*

This inspired other research showing that the brain, however important, is not the only control center of the body. In the gut, brain-like networks of interconnected, multilayered neurons are able to effectively control the gut even without any input from the brain. In fact, somewhere between 90% and 95% of the serotonin in the body—a neurotransmitter linked to treatments for depression—is produced, transported, and utilized in this "gut brain."

This is part of an emerging understanding that the brain, the autonomic nervous system that controls body processes such as breathing and heart rate, the endocrine system, and the immune system work together as an interactive whole. The brain is important, of course, and it may in many ways be the team captain, but the team members participate in management.

With all of this evidence, you might think it would start a revolution in neuroscience—a race to discover how brain-like processes throughout the biology of the body help to create the mind. So far, this hasn't happened. That the brain creates the mind is still the operating assumption. But in light of more recent findings in neuroscience, this is clearly only part of the story.

One of the main reasons neuroscientists believe the brain creates the mind is because damage to the brain often affect mental functioning. Of course, a brain is necessary for the mind to function, but so are a heart and liver. Keep in mind that neurotransmitters were called *brain chemicals* for decades *simply because no one thought to look for them outside of the brain*. So it is possible that little evidence has been found for the role of other parts of the body because there has been little effort to look.

A story is told of a man down on his knees under a street lamp, feeling around on the pavement with his hands. A woman walking by asks him what he is looking for. "My keys," he replies.

"How did you lose them?" she asks.

The man points to a car parked in the shadows across the street and says, "I dropped them over there."

"Why aren't you looking over there?" the woman asks.

He replies, "Because this is where I can see."

The tools of cognitive neuroscience are designed to look for relationships between brain activity and behavior, based on deep-seated assumptions about where the mind resides, and what is important to measure. To some degree, what such tools can measure shapes the kinds of research questions that are commonly asked.

Another subtle factor that may contribute to the lack of interest in looking beyond the brain may be the fact that a scientific education is also an induction into a head-located attentional stance. As noted in an earlier chapter, there is evidence that locating oneself in the head improves intellectual skills—so this is a useful adaptation. However, the sense that "I" am located in my head, even if not noticed, subtly supports the belief that the mind is in the brain.

Of course, the mind cannot be directly measured or detected scientifically. Medically, if a person does not respond to being shaken or called loudly, they are considered to be unconscious. But there is no medical or scientific device that can detect mind. Instruments can measure brain activity, just as they can measure blood pressure, but not mind. So there is no direct scientific evidence that the mind is in the brain or any other specific location in the body.

It was this kind of dubious reasoning that behaviorists of the early twentieth century, such as John Watson, used to dismiss the idea of a human mind as completely unnecessary. As late as the 1950s, B. F. Skinner, the leading behaviorist of his era, was still trying to build a psychology that explained everything humans do as nothing more than mindless responses to their environment.

In 1959, Noam Chomsky—now one of the most honored linguists, philosophers, and cognitive scientists of the twentieth century—argued that human language shows a creativity well beyond what can be explained as responses to inputs. In other words, our capacity for the creative use of language only makes sense if humans have minds. Chomsky's work made it acceptable for psychology to assume people actually have minds. Yet science is no closer to clearly defining what a mind is or how it can be measured than it was a hundred years ago.

When you have fully experienced moving your attention from the head down to the space of the belly, this experience may make it easier to imagine that the mind is the intelligence of the entire human being, and is produced by the whole body. As I've noted, moving your attention to the belly does not mean that your brain is no longer participating and that you are relying on neurons in your gut. Far from it. Your brain is intimately involved in the creation of the felt sense that your internal location has shifted. But it does point to the aliveness and intelligence that permeates the entire body.

After experiencing the shift of attention into the body, Rania, a graduate student studying to become a psychotherapist, acknowledged that, "although I had noticed my body in other meditation exercises and bodily experiences, I never had the experience of having my attention move to another part of my body. This brought me into an entirely different kind of transpersonal experience. The idea of the mind and body being one organism didn't make sense until I had this experience."

The work of Dr. Antonio Damasio shows that the mind relies in part on information processed in parts of the body other than the brain. Somewhat by accident, Damasio found that a certain kind of brain damage impacts mental functioning because the brain has lost access to emotional marker signals generated elsewhere in the body. These signals inform the brain about what the body has learned from previous experiences. Without this information, the speed and quality of decision-making is severely impaired, even though skills related to language, reason, problem solving, memory, and attention are unaffected.

To summarize, the neurotransmitters that are believed to be responsible for creating mental experience are located throughout the body. Some parts of the body, such as the gut, can manage complex operations without any input from the brain. Some parts of the body outside of the brain learn from past experience and relay this information to the brain. Why then is the mind almost exclusively ascribed to the activity of the brain?

The brain is an important vital organ and deserves all the attention it gets in neuroscience research. But as a term, *brain* is also used to refer to the aspect of the body that produces the mind. For example, a word such as *brainpower* uses the term brain as a metaphor, to point to the mental ability that the brain creates. In this metaphorical sense, if the whole body participates in creating the mind, it may be possible to begin to think in terms of a *whole-body brain.*

One of the challenges of expanding to a whole-person neuroscience is that current research methods are mostly designed to study the organ that sits in the head. It will take time to develop new research methods that can look at how other kinds of neural activity throughout the body may correlate with mental experience as well. These efforts will be spurred forward as neuroscience begins to ask *whole-person research questions* about the mind, rather than mainly *brain questions.*

The prospect of a whole-person neuroscience points to what may be an entirely new frontier in the study of mind, consciousness, and psychology. Brain science was revolutionized in 1929 when Hans Berger discovered he could measure electrical activity from the brain by placing electrodes on the head. It was revolutionized again in 1991, when fMRI techniques were developed that could measure in real time the structures of the brain that were activated under various conditions. When neural activity throughout the body can be measured with similar precision, it may transform cognitive neuroscience into a truly whole-person discipline.

11.

THE CORE OF YOUR BEING

The core is power, inspiration, motivation, and charisma —or "rizz." When you feel moved by a speech or book or movie to do something great or worthy, your attention has been pulled into core. Core is a key element of performance, public speaking, and personal presence. Core is the attentional posture that great art inspires. It is very like the state created by *shamatha* practice, which, along with vipassana, is a key part of Buddhist mindfulness.

When my daughter was around ten years old, I took her to a Tom Petty concert. The show opened with a warm-up band of skilled musicians playing well-written songs, but as I listened to them, I thought to myself, "I could just as well be home listening to the radio." They tried hard, but there was no juice, no electricity, no sparkle. Then the house lights went down, and out of the darkness came a voice: "Good evening." A ripple ran through my body. That was Tom Petty —he was at core, and *my core responded.*

Whether or not they have words for it, each member of an audience knows when a performer connects. That evening, Tom Petty connected. Halfway through the concert, Tom announced that one of the Heartbreakers was going to perform his own song. Tom stepped back and played in the band as his bandmate rendered well-crafted verses to a thoroughly warmed audience. The performance was top notch—but there was no magic. *I could not feel the singer connecting with me.*

This skill is challenging to describe because it is wordless and invisible to the eye. Many of those who have the ability to move an audience can only describe how they do it using metaphors, because they have no language for the underlying process. Yet it is a skill that can make the difference between success and failure as a performer—or in any role that requires inspiring a group of people.

When you are at core, your attention sits at the centerline of your body, as if right along the front of your spine. One of the things that makes being at core effective for being in front of people is that it provides a way to handle the gaze of the audience. Anyone who has tried public speaking knows the feeling when all the eyes turn to you. The sheer energy of that collective gaze makes the heart pound and the stomach quiver.

Yet at core, the energy of all those eyes is much easier to tolerate. At core, you can receive the power of that gaze and allow it to amplify your own presence. If your core were a glowing line of light, you can imagine that as you feel the energy from all that attention flow into your core, it makes your core shine that much brighter—and you radiate that presence back out to the audience.

In a session with Jim Nabors—a television star and singer from the 1960s to early 2000s—he shared with me that a man claiming to be able to measure the energy coming from people's bodies had hooked him up to a measuring device while Nabors was performing in front of an audience. Afterwards he reported to Nabors that there was so much energy coming off of his body while he was singing that it was literally off the charts on his device. When you are at core, you can let in the attention of the audience so that the energy you radiate back to them is far beyond what you could generate on your own.

You do not need to be a performer to benefit from being at core. An inspiring speaker can make you feel motivated, but you can generate your own motivation by being at core. A legendary artist may move stadium-sized crowds, but you can use this attentional stance to increase your impact even if your audience is a volleyball team that you coach, a small team at work, or your own young children.

Focused Mindfulness

This at-core attentional posture also has similarity with the Buddhist mindfulness practice of shamatha. Shamatha is associated with bliss and with a highly focused attentional state. In this quality of sharp mental focus, shamatha differs from the vipassana state discussed in Chapter 9.

From our study measuring the brain activity associated with different attentional stances, we found that the stance of being at core was associated with several positive emotional states, which we interpreted as equivalent to bliss. We also found that the highest levels of neural arousal (associated with the ability to focus attention) in the *beta* and *gamma* frequency bands were all associated with attentional stances focused at the core of the body.

Together, these pieces of evidence led us to suggest that the attentional stance of focus at the centerline of the body appeared to be quite similar to the state produced by the Buddhist practice of shamatha.

Here is how to create this At-Core attentional stance:

FIND YOUR CORE, BE YOUR CORE: THE AT-CORE STANCE
(FIG. 11.1)

Touch gently on the center of the chest, then lift the finger. Notice the sensation on the skin that stays after you lift the touch. Feel the sensation and imagine that it slides slowly back towards your spine, until it bumps into the front of your spine. If it helps, you can imagine the sensation as a point of light.

Imagine that you are this focused point deep in the center of the chest, a point that feels itself. Imagine that the sounds around you arrive here, that you are this point in the chest that received the air as you draw each breath—that the air comes right through the wall of your chest and through your upper back, and then slides out again as you release the breath.

If any part of you is aware of the point "down there" in your chest, invite it to melt and flow down into the center of the chest, into the point that feels itself here in the chest.

Now imagine that instead of a sensation or a point of light, you are a small pot of golden, radiant honey right here in the center of the chest.

Imagine that the pot of honey tips over, and the glowing honey begins to flow down the front of your spine. Allow yourself to flow down with the honey, along the front of your spine.

Allow yourself to extend all the way down the spine to the base of your pelvis. Feel yourself as a sensation or line of glowing light from the center of the chest all the way to the base of the pelvis.

Notice the sounds around you, and receive them here, at the centerline of your body. Be the core of the body that feels itself, that receives the sensations of the body, that draws and releases each breath.

Figure 11.1

The distance from the chest to the pelvis is just a small part of the core, but it is enough to practice with. Repeat this first core exercise several times a day for three or four days before adding the following steps:

> Feel yourself at the front of your spine in your chest and abdomen. Now imagine that your spine extends down about 5 or 6 feet (1½ m) further, about 20 inches (50 cm) below the ground if you were standing up.

> Imagine that you can allow yourself to slowly extend down along this extra portion of your spine, just a few inches or centimeters at a time, until you reach the end of this imaginary spine. Imagine you can anchor yourself here, as if you can make a solid connection here.

Again, practice extending your core downward in this way several times a day for at least two days before adding this final step. It is okay if you can only bring your awareness part of the way along your imaginary extension:

> Feel yourself sitting at the front of your spine from the center of the chest all the way down the extension you are adding to your spine in your imagination, or as far down as you can.

> Now imagine that you can allow yourself to extend upward as well, just a little at a time. Feel as though your line of sensation or light grows upward

through the chest, up through the centerline of your neck, and up into the center of your head.

Finally, imagine that you can allow yourself to extend upward through the top of your head, up a foot or more (½ m) above the top of your head.

Imagine you can feel yourself sitting as a line of sensation or a line of light from below your pelvis to above your head. Be this line through your center that feels the whole length of itself.

Figure 11.2

Being at the core *feels great.* It is a stance of quiet power but not puffed up with self-importance. It is a stance of mental clarity that includes the body senses of intuition. It is a stance of fearlessness that can be present to tremors of uneasiness in the stomach without giving in to their anxieties. It is a clear-eyed confidence that sees the opening, senses the risks, and navigates without quavering. It exhilarates without tipping into over-confidence or hubris.

The first attentional stance introduced in this book was how to create a quietly focused mind. Being at core extends this quiet state of the intellectual mind into a focused state of your whole body's intelligence. At core, your thinking and feeling capacities learn to work together in a synergy that opens a deeper and wiser way of knowing, discerning directions, and making decisions.

I began Chapter 1 with my experiment of trying to find out what made famous people famous, and that moment in the theater in San Francisco when the great actor Richard Burton raised his arm, spoke the last line of the play, and I *felt* his presence as it rolled up through the space of the whole theater. I did not have the language for it then, but that was the moment he moved into his core.

Learning to sit in this attentional stance will not make you famous, of course. But it can help you become more effective, more focused, and more productive. It can increase the impact you have on others, whether you are speaking to a group or in a private conversation. Your attentional stance doesn't just affect your internal state, it transmits to those around you and impacts their experience of you.

As you become confident with this practice, you can begin by simply imagining a line of sensation or light along the front of your spine in the chest and belly, then allowing your sense of self to come in and become that line. You become the line that notices itself, and that receives the information from each of your senses. From the centerline of the chest and belly, you can allow your line of attention to extend downward and then upward.

I encourage you to weave this practice into your daily life. Bring yourself to core as you start your day. Come to core again before each new task and challenge, or when you feel a moment of worry or discouragement. Bring yourself back to core as you come home from work or errands.

If you find you are not yet able to feel the core below the pelvis or above the head, relax. Be the core as far as it will extend and practice sitting there, trusting that one day you will notice that another door opens, and you can extend farther.

As you will learn in the next chapter, when you combine this state with the warm presence of gratitude in the space of the belly, the two balance each other: acceptance and motivation that move in harmony.

Figure 11.3

12.

Whole-Person Presence

Presence is the experience of "this is my mind." Presence shapes the quality of your present-moment experience of yourself. It is not just a product of your attitude and skills, or even that you sit or stand in a certain way. It is an invisible language that is part of every conversation, every meeting, and every interaction. It is the quality that seems to radiate out from your body, a felt presence that others experience—often without noticing it—and that informs others about you. Presence is also what lets you connect intimately with others, whether in a personal conversation over coffee, or in a presentation to a thousand people.

When attention sits in the head, presence is dimmed, and its quality does not invite connection. I walked into a store that sold barbecue grills, willing to be convinced if I saw an amazing deal. A salesman spotted me and scurried over. He was a tall man, with his attention firmly in his head. As he made his sales pitch, his presence felt harsh. Because it came from attention that was seated in his head, it seemed like he was talking down to me, as if there was a too-bright spotlight mounted on his head. Even though he seemed sincere and entirely professional, I excused myself as quickly as possible and practically ran from the store. The quality of his presence drove me out.

You may have had the experience of going to meet with a friend or colleague with the intention of sharing some personal concern, only to find that as you sit across from them, your desire to talk about it has vanished. It just does not feel right to bring it up. If your would-be listener is in their head, their presence is filled with their own thoughts instead of attending to you.

On the other hand, you might sit down with someone intending to make small talk, and suddenly find you are sharing the secrets of your soul. You might be in love—or you may have found a listener who knows how to sit in their body and use presence to create a safe container. When presence comes from attention that is fully in the body, it can be magnetic and compelling.

Ray Walker, one of the Jordanaires who sang backup vocals for Elvis Presley during the 1950s and 1960s, shared a story about Elvis on a radio interview. Though he did not use the term, it was about the presence that Elvis carried. As he told it, Ray and about fifteen others from the crew were standing backstage hanging out and shooting the breeze, twenty or thirty feet from the loading dock. All at once, as if on cue, every one of them fell silent and turned on their heels to face the loading dock. Just then Elvis opened the door and walked in. He said nothing, but the sheer power of his presence compelled them to drop their conversation and turn to look in his direction, *even before he opened the door.*

There are performers who use presence in a way that shows they understand exactly what they are doing. I attended a concert of the Rolling Stones "No Security" tour, bringing along my daughter and my partner. This was the first Stones concert for my daughter, now a teenager, and I knew she was excited to see them live. But the first two sets were a disappointment. Their technique was excellent, as always, but the magic wasn't there. We later discovered that their very next concert date was cancelled due to Mick Jagger's illness—so he may have been coming down with something that evening.

Yet it was what Jagger did in the third set that caught my attention. During one of the numbers, it looked as if he was pulling something invisible up from the ground underneath him, again and again. After each pull, he stood as if he were holding a huge invisible beachball, much bigger than his body, and hurled it at a different part of the arena. I wondered whether he might be doing something about the lack of presence in the concert, but I knew this would be expecting too much.

Then it was our turn. Jagger reached down toward the ground, drew himself up as if drawing a great unseen ball from the ground beneath him, and heaved it straight at us. When it hit, my sense of connection with the music and the band changed instantly. *I felt them*, in the way that I had come to expect of great performers generally, and the Rolling Stones in particular. I realized that Mick Jagger knew *exactly* what he was doing with presence.

Presence is the magic that a great performer brings, but it is also the invisible power that helps a business leader hold an audience, negotiate effectively, lead a team meeting, and inspire employees. It is the quality in a teacher that empowers students to do their best work. It is what experienced coaches, therapists, and consultants use to create a comfortable connection so their clients can speak authentically. Presence is the *silent, invisible "something"* that, when shaped by the right attentional stance, turns competence into consistent peak performance.

Helen, the executive coach from the first chapter, learned to use presence to create a more comfortable and connected coaching space. Presence invites rapport, a sense that it is safe to say what is actually true. Coaching, counseling, and consulting all work more effectively when a client can be transparent about what is going on with them and what their needs are, and can remain receptive to unexpected or uncomfortable insights.

Great art can have a presence of its own as well. When I was a teenager, I had the good fortune of travelling to the Netherlands with classmates and visiting the Rijksmuseum, which houses many works by the masterful seventeenth-century Dutch painter, Rembrandt van Rijn. Walking through gallery after gallery, I could see that Rembrandt's works carried a special golden glow, but I took in this fact as no more than a curiosity—the way one might notice the presence or absence of a pickle with their hamburger.

Swinging around a corner, I came face to face with *The Night Watch*, a roughly 3.5m x 4m painting by Rembrandt of a Dutch civil guard company. There was nothing in this image of officers and guardsmen from more than three centuries ago that meant anything to me. Yet I felt frozen to the floor, the beauty of the piece bringing tears to my eyes. It was a moment that forever changed my relationship with art, for I realized that art can carry qualities that inspire, that heal, and that transform.

I cannot explain exactly how physical objects can carry qualities of presence, but it is my experience that they do. I was in New Delhi, India, for a conference, and a colleague suggested a trip by taxi to see the Taj Mahal. I had seen travel posters of this magnificent building since I was young, and I did not want to pass up the opportunity to see it for myself.

Our taxi ride lasted nearly two hours, and after that we had to walk some ways on foot. As we strolled down a covered portico, we caught our first view of the gleaming white marble structure. Soon we were directly in front of the building and began our approach down the wide walkways leading to and from its entrance. It was farther than it looked, and the sun was hot, so we were glad for some shelter as we climbed shaded stairs to the platform on which the temple-like structure stood, and then entered its airy interior.

Before my visit I had not paid much attention to what kind of building the Taj Mahal was. I had imagined that it must serve some religious purpose. On entering it, I saw two stone tombs in the center. My colleague explained that here lay the bodies of the great seventeenth-century Mughal emperor Shah Jahan, alongside his favorite wife, Mumtaz Mahal. Coincidentally, this mausoleum was finished just one year after Rembrandt completed painting *The Night Watch*.

As we walked the circle that surrounded the two stone coffins in the center of the hall, my colleague said, "I feel something here." We stopped, and I attended to the sensations in my body. We agreed that the quality was grief. I suggested that we continue circling the tombs to see whether the intensity changed. As we neared the entrance, the feeling of grief grew steadily stronger. By walking back and forth across the entrance, we both concluded that the sensation was strongest just a few feet—about a meter— outside of the entrance to the mausoleum.

Upon returning to New Delhi, we did some reading about the Taj Mahal and discovered that after the body of Mumtaz Mahal was entombed here, the emperor Shah Jahan came to the mausoleum every day, stood in front of the door, and wept. Neither my colleague nor I knew this story before we visited the Taj Mahal, yet the place where we felt this quality of grief most keenly was exactly the place where

Shah Jahan stood, more than three and a half centuries before, and poured out his grief for the loss of his beloved.

Something similar can happen in churches, shrines, and temples where people have prayed or meditated for centuries. Perhaps there is something about their qualities of presence that creates this sense that the air itself is somehow quiet, and quieting, for those who visit.

Now that you have a sense of what presence is and how it can impact your skills and relationships, it is time to cultivate your own presence. This is not about your attitude, your posture, your beliefs about yourself, or the words you say. It is all about your attentional stance.

In Chapter 9, you discovered how to become the attentional stance in the space of the belly and generate the kind of low arousal positive affect state associated with mindfulness and life satisfaction. Chapter 11 added to this the attentional stance of being focused at the core of the body. When these two are practiced together, the result is whole-person presence.

Before trying this, you should practice the exercises in Chapters 9 and 11 several times a day for at least two weeks. With these skills in place, here is how to create your own powerful presence:

WHOLE-PERSON PRESENCE (FIG. 12.1)

Notice the space inside your belly. Imagine the spreading warmth of gratitude is bubbling up in the area of your heart, and allow this warmth to flow down the front of your spine, into the space of the belly. Imagine that as it flows down into the belly, you flow with it.

As you become the space of the belly, allow the warmth from the heart to fill the belly from the bottom, first up to the level of the navel, then all the way up to the stomach.

Be the space of the belly that feels itself, that receives the sounds around you, that notices the sensations of the body, that draws and releases the breath right through the wall of the abdomen and through the low back. Be the contentment.

Now imagine that the warmth along the front of the spine forms into a line of focused attention rising out of the space of the belly. Imagine that your attention is like mercury in an old-fashioned thermometer that rises out of the warm roundness of the belly into a straight line along the front of the spine.

Imagine that your spine extends downward from your pelvis another 5 or 6 feet (1½ m), and imagine that you can feel your core attention flowing down that extended spine just a little at a time at a time, until you reach the end.

Be the space of the space of the belly that feels itself, and be the focused core that extends from your heart to below your feet. Imagine that your core can extend upward from the heart, along the front of your spine, through the center of your head, and straight up several feet (1 m) above the top of your head.

Be the space of the belly, warm and receptive, and be the core, focused and clear. Imagine that the radiance shining from the belly and from the core blend together, filling the space of your body and the space around you, out to several feet (1 m) in every direction.

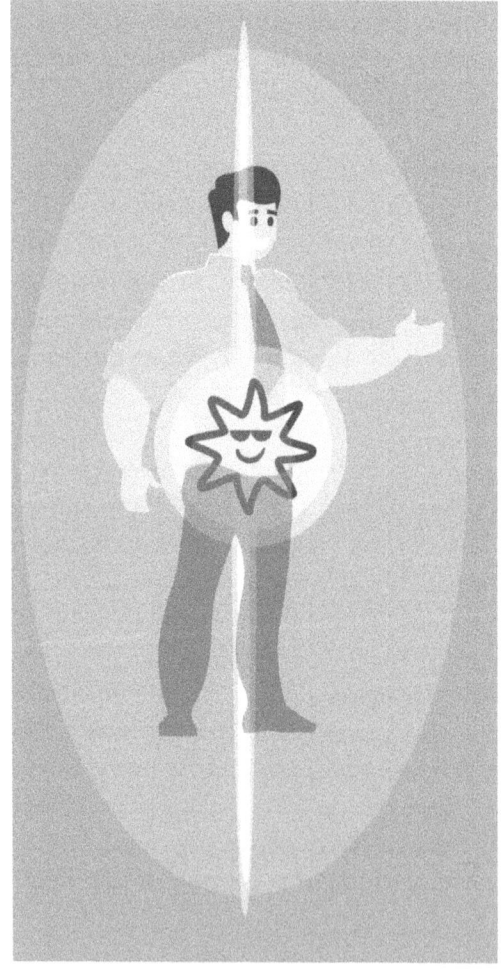

Figure 12.1

If you can only feel to the surface of your skin, this is fine. Allow the radiance in your belly and the brightness of your core to fill the space of your body to its edges. Trust that as you practice coming to the edge of your felt space, it will open and allow you to feel more in time.

One might note that it has taken a whole book to get to this point, but it is worth remembering that *it has only taken one book to show you the way to this state.* If you were learning this in one-on-one instruction, it might take just a few hours. Before the development of these Attention Strategies, *no other step-by-step tools existed that would empower you to attain this advanced state in such a short time.*

You might notice that this stance of whole person presence brings together the two stances identified as most similar to two important forms of Buddhist practice: vipassana and shamatha. Of course, approaching these states from psychology will always be different than if one is doing a Buddhist practice. Buddhist states can only be achieved by practicing Buddhism. But it is interesting to note that of the attentional stances we tested, the two stances most similar to traditional descriptions from Buddhist writings are the two most strongly associated with positive emotions, and the two key contributors to whole-person presence. This seems unlikely to be accident or coincidence.

A graduate student studying to be a psychotherapist in a Buddhist-informed degree program said:

Attentional stances seem to capture and translate for Western minds what many ancient Buddhist and mindfulness practices are attempting to convey. Though I had been practicing meditation and yoga for many years before beginning this class, and working with a very wise teacher and mentor from a Tibetan Buddhist lineage, I did not fully—in an embodied way—understand what was meant by "being with your breathing" or "being in your heart." Like many Westerners, I was so stuck in my head that I believed that sensing the sensations of my breathing from my self-location in my head was what I was supposed to do.

In this way, attentional stances can be of use to those who wish to engage in traditional practices as well as those who want to benefit from similar practices without aligning with a spiritual tradition.

Whatever uses you may find for this state of whole-person presence, it is just the beginning of a journey into discovering and unpacking the resources that you have within your own mind and presence. You have walked through the door to a new way of being. The Epilogue will give you just a taste of what awaits you there.

Epilogue: Where to Now?

Now that you have experienced Attention Strategies, you know for yourself how you can drop quickly into a more natural, embodied state. This state is not magical or mystical or spiritual—though some states may support access to those types of experience. Although embodiment is unusual in Western culture, it is not in any way extraordinary. It is simply more authentic, and more *you*.

When compared with the busy everyday mind, this natural way of being allows you to hold a more powerful presence, sharpen personal and professional skills, and connect more deeply and authentically in relationships. It allows you to be in the world more effectively, more intelligently, more elegantly, and more successfully. But these changes are not extraordinary—they are capacities that are yours naturally when you release yourself from the limits of your everyday mind.

As with any muscle, the "muscle" of attention becomes stronger as you practice over time. With practice, you will see that what you have learned in this book is just the beginning. As you step through the door that these exercises open, you will find that the space within you extends farther than your imagination can reach.

Closer at hand there are extensions of the practices you already know.

You have learned how to be at core, and you know that performers and leaders use this stance in order to be effective. But there are specific, professional-level strategies that will invisibly increase your impact when speaking in public, performing, or giving a presentation.

You have learned how to cultivate your whole-person presence, but if you work with people individually, either as a therapist, coach, or consultant, there are precise ways to build on the attentional stance of whole-person presence and create a felt quality of safety and connection with another person. You can learn how to wordlessly invite your client into co-creating an atmosphere that encourages trust and transparency.

You may be acquainted with the Enneagram, a personality system based on nine types. When you discover the Attention Strategy that each of these types uses, you will open your ability to recognize these kinds of response in yourself and others, and to benefit from the gifts of your type while letting go of the pitfalls.

Beyond this are skills for awakening and sharpening intuition, for deep psychological healing, and for opening your perceptions to the subtle nuances that provide insight into how relationships work. Whole-person presence is itself a powerful tool that can change your experience of life. But it is only the first step in a wholly new way of living.

REFERENCES

Chapter 3

Sester, M. (2022). When the self dwells in the heart: How a heart-located attentional stance facilitates a felt sense of connection [Doctoral dissertation]. California Institute of Integral Studies.

Fetterman, A. K., & Robinson, M. D. (2013). Do you use your head or follow your heart? Self-location predicts personality, emotion, decision making, and performance. *Journal of Personality and Social Psychology, 105*(2), 316-334.

Chapter 5

Gendlin, E. T. (1999). A new model. *Journal of Consciousness Studies, 6*(2-3), 232-237.

Porges, S. W. (2009). The polyvagal theory: New insights into adaptive reactions of the autonomic nervous system. *Cleveland Clinic Journal of Medicine, 76* (Suppl 2), S86.

Hartelius, G., Likova, L. T., & Tyler, C. W. (2022). Self-regulation of seat of attention into various attentional stances facilitates access to cognitive and emotional resources: An EEG study. *Frontiers in Psychology, 13*, 810780.

Likova, L. T., & Tyler, C. W. (2008). Occipital network for figure/ground organization. *Experimental Brain Research, 189*, 257-267.

Chapter 7

Marolt-Sender, M. A. (2014). A phenomenological inquiry into the attention postures of flow-like states [Doctoral dissertation]. Institute of Transpersonal Psychology.

Chapter 8

Smith, G. P., & Hartelius, G. (2020). Resolution of dissociated ego states relieves flashback-related symptoms in combat-related PTSD: A brief mindfulness based intervention. *Military Psychology, 32*(2), 135-148.

Chapter 9

Fröber, K., & Dreisbach, G. (2012). How positive affect modulates proactive control: Reduced usage of informative cues under positive affect with low arousal. *Frontiers in Psychology, 3,* 265.

McManus, M. D., Siegel, J. T., & Nakamura, J. (2019). The predictive power of low-arousal positive affect. *Motivation and Emotion, 43,* 130-144.

Hartelius, G., Likova, L. T., & Tyler, C. W. (2023). Self-regulation of attentional stance facilitates induction of meditative states. *Electronic Imaging, 35,* 1-8.

Chapter 10

Chomsky, N. (1959). Chomsky, N. 1959. A review of B. F. Skinner's *Verbal behavior. Language, 35*(1), 26–58.

Bechara, A., & Damasio, A. R. (2005). The somatic marker hypothesis: A neural theory of economic decision. *Games and Economic Behavior, 52*(2), 336-372.

Pert, C. B. (2010). *Molecules of emotion: The science behind mind-body medicine.* Simon and Schuster.

Pert, C. B., Dreher, H. E., & Ruff, M. R. (1998). The psychosomatic network: foundations of mind-body medicine. *Alternative Therapies in Health and Medicine, 4*(4), 30-41.

Chapter 11

Hartelius, G., Likova, L. T., & Tyler, C. W. (2023). Self-regulation of attentional stance facilitates induction of meditative states. *Electronic Imaging, 35,* 1-8.

ABOUT THE AUTHORS

GLENN HARTELIUS, PHD, is an internationally known scholar and thought leader in integral and transpersonal psychology who has recently been honored with the Abraham Maslow Award, one of the highest distinctions bestowed by the American Psychological Association. As director of Attention Strategies Institute, he conducts grant-funded research into novel aspects of consciousness. Through his role as director of a PhD program at the California Institute for Human Sciences, he mentors university students for the next generation of scholars in the use of a whole-person approach that includes powerful and often neglected aspects of who we are.

MICHAELA AIZER, CHT, has been a transformative educational activist for more than 40 years as a counselor, teacher, public speaker, organizer, and mentor. As co-creator of the Attention Strategies work, she brings her lifelong commitment to personal transformation and focus on authentic communication, respect for individual world-views, and celebration of community as a creative and healing force.

www.ingramcontent.com/pod-product-compliance
Lightning Source LLC
Chambersburg PA
CBHW051212120626
46547CB00013B/1318
* 9 7 9 8 9 8 9 7 7 5 6 4 4 *